KICK THE SHIT
Out of Social Anxiety

Breaking Free of the Socially Distanced Self

KICK THE SHIT
Out of Social Anxiety

Breaking Free of the Socially Distanced Self

Lee Vallely

ISBN (paperback): 979-8-9916005-0-7
ISBN (ebook): 979-8-9916005-1-4

Book design and production by www.AuthorSuccess.com

Printed in the United States of America

Contents

"There is nothing either good or bad,
but thinking makes it so."[1]

WILLIAM SHAKESPEARE

Giggling and crouching behind the cream leather-like sofa, convinced that they have no idea that I'm there, I hear the familiar voices of my family. My uncle then announces, "Ladies and gentlemen, the moment you have all been waiting for! Here he is . . . Mister . . . Lee . . . Vallely!"

I burst out from behind the couch, wiggling my hips and singing in my three-year-old voice.

That's one of my first memories of being a confident, fun-loving child.

I was so confident, especially in my brown suit, which was my, and obviously everyone else's, favorite. I even had a "got my brown suit on, I'm so cool" walk. I loved talking, singing, and dancing and was pretty full of myself. Why shouldn't I be? I was great.

Then I got quieter and quieter until there were times when I didn't talk at all, never wanting to be noticed. In fact, people often thought I was perhaps bordering on autistic. I could hardly string a sentence together when I was around people I didn't know.

I became shy. Not born shy, as demonstrated by my phenomenal performance that possibly rivaled Elvis Presley. I learned to be shy.

Growing up in what was, in my experience, a very racist and violent area of Birmingham, England, and having so many conflicting views of life and of how to be, I developed limiting beliefs, also known as BS (belief systems, but bullshit works too).

My grandfather was from Bangladesh, which made me a quarter cast Bengali. I didn't know anything about the culture or the language. I never even met my grandfather. I did get a tan though, which I can now appreciate, though it was not so good in the environment I lived in as a child. I was spat at and called grotesque names—I was even punched in the face by one adult and kicked like a dog by another, which was what the adult called me. And after all this abuse, I didn't even inherit the customary corner grocery shop. That's an English joke. No? Okay, moving on.

I grew up feeling like a low life, trying to stay out of the sun in case I got darker. I lied constantly about my heritage, even at such a young age. I felt worthless, scared, and a fraud. This created such deep limiting beliefs (BS) that became reinforced as time went on.

A family member, who I was absolutely petrified of at the time, made a flippant statement that changed the trajectory of my life. Had anyone else said it, or in a different context, it may not have had anywhere near the effect it had. But this "terrifying" person was mad at me because I was constantly asking questions. On this occasion, as we were watching TV, I was asking, "Who's that? What do they do? Why is the sky blue?" And so on. I can appreciate how annoying that must have been sometimes. Why is the sky blue BTW?

They shouted, "If you don't have anything important to say, don't say anything!"

My mouth zipped shut.

Think about that statement. Even as an adult, let alone a young kid, how do you work out what's important to say or not? From then on, I doubted pretty much every word I spoke, and, as a consequence, I rarely spoke.

It's hard to even imagine myself back then compared to now—a very scared, confused boy who didn't know who he was, what he stood for, or even what was the right or wrong way to be. I had conflicting information from influential people, so it was a scary and very confusing time. I had a constant, deep, and heavy feeling like I didn't belong, and consequently, I didn't, because my energy (and my resting bitch face) would keep people away. No matter where I was, I felt like I should be somewhere else.

My biggest fear of all, almost to the point of being a phobia, was of being rejected or embarrassed socially. That feeling stayed with me for decades, and what's weird is that I seemed to put myself in scenarios that created even more fear and not belonging.

Ever notice how our lives seem to fit with what we believe about ourselves? I was awkward, trying to fit into a mold that wasn't created for me, trying to be a tough guy, yet in my heart, I was a geek. I played it off well, though. I got good at playing tough.

The truth was that I was more scared of what might happen to me if I told this family member that I'd lost a fight or been scared than I was of the person I was fighting. I was a geek, but that didn't really fly in the world I was living in. So, I created some crazy belief systems (BS). And still, to this day, I'm finding and gradually letting go of the crazy ones that hold me back.

Everyone experiences stress and anxiety at some point in their lives.

According to the Anxiety and Depression Association of America (ADAA), anxiety disorders are the most common mental illness in the USA, affecting 40 million adults eighteen and over every year.[2]

Social anxiety is the second most commonly diagnosed mental health disorder in the Western world, affecting almost everyone in some way, at some time in their lives, meaning that the actual number of people suffering from social (or any form of) anxiety is probably way higher than that, since a lot of people, including myself, do not get diagnosed. But that doesn't count for the millions and possibly billions who have a general fear of socializing; of life itself. Not a full-blown phobia, but still debilitating and experienced regularly. It's very common for this to lead to general anxiety, depression, and substance use disorder. Most people won't have a full-blown phobia, but will feel social pressure and awkwardness daily. Remember this can be hidden by years of thinking that it's natural to feel this angst in the pit of your stomach, which is understandable since it is a primal instinct to fit in socially. In Paleolithic times or thereabouts, if you were cast out by the "tribe," you were unlikely to survive the night. A bit like Birmingham.

But forget statistics, we want to address you and how this affects you. Most people not only live in a state of "fear and anxiety," but they're not even aware of it because it feels "normal."

The most common coping mechanism seems to be drugs and alcohol. But this is something outside of us and can only ever offer temporary relief and seriously debilitating side effects.

We all have some fear of being rejected. It's almost built into our system. Although most people don't dwell on it, some don't even realize or acknowledge that it's a problem. People believe it's natural, but I'm going to show you in this book that it *is* normal, due to conditioning, but it is not natural!

I will show you how to get back to your natural state, which is something that you may have only had glimpses of in the past.

Who would've thought that Oprah—yes, Oprah—is introverted and suffered from anxiety? Obviously, she has extroverted tendencies, but in order to recharge her batteries, she needs to "cocoon," in her own words. She overcame her anxieties by using the energy as fuel for her drive for success.[3] Dan Harris, author of the book *10% Happier*, had a panic attack on live TV. Good place to have one.[4] Beyonce is introverted, so she uses an alter ego, which we will address in this book, to be the amazing person that we see in her performances. Adele overcomes her anxiety by imagining what Beyonce would do in her place.

It's not just introverts that suffer from anxiety, though it tends to be more obvious as a social anxiety. Extroverts (very few are just one or the other) can suffer the same anxiety, but it will be labeled differently and dealt with differently, too.

So many people, including, if not especially, a lot of successful and famous people, suffer in silence, thinking it's just a part of life. There are a plethora of medications and therapies to help with both severe and milder cases of anxiety, but what if there was a fundamental flaw in the way we think about this "disease of the mind?" What if our experience of life was being created from the inside out, not from outside circumstances?

Fear and excitement have similar physical responses. The only difference is the way we breathe and the meaning that we give to the feeling. All anxiety can be traced back to the meaning that we give to our feelings in the moment. Of course, if hearing that is all you need (maybe it is), then you wouldn't really bother reading this book. If I said to one hundred socially anxious people that the reason that they are suffering is not because of their circumstances, but how they feel about those circumstances, I bet that ninety-nine would understand and agree with me. This is not a real statistic so don't quote me on this, but from my experience most sufferers would agree.

So why do they continue suffering? Why did I?

The reason is that there is a humungous difference between intellectually understanding and experientially knowing.

The plus side of my (in my mind) yucky upbringing is that it gave me an insatiable appetite for learning. Predominantly learning psychology, then positive psychology and neurolinguistic programming (co-founded by John Grinder and one of my favorite mentors, Richard Bandler),[5] so that I could figure out how to "fix me." Told you I was a geek. And, no question, I did make some positive changes, albeit temporarily.

But it wasn't until I understood what I'm sharing with you in this book that my bullshit past no longer had its hold on me.

There's a life-changing analogy I heard from one of my mentors, Michael Neill, author of many bestselling books including *The Inside-Out Revolution*.[6] It's the basis for where we're going in this book. You may have heard of the idea that we are a diamond in the rough. A lot of people have said that. But what does being the diamond mean? And what's the rough?

The metaphor we are using is that we are a diamond, covered in shit (alias BS [belief systems]), traumas, and doubts that we paint over to imitate the diamond.

The diamond in this metaphor is our innate well-being, our true self. Our true self is whole and perfect, unblemished, like the metaphorical diamond. You could say your inner being or your higher self, whatever word works for you because it's pointing in the same direction.

It's the innocent child singing with no inhibitions, fear, or lack of confidence . . .

So, if we are so perfect, why do we suffer so much?

Because our diamond is covered in shit belief systems! The shit is the rough. The name of this book is *Kick the Shit Out of...* I don't do this just to be crude (although that may be a bonus), I do this to emphasize how much of a role this plays in our lives, and once we realize it, the power and the illusion fall away. We can kick that shit out of the way of our lives!

We can only see the diamond from inside out. There is nothing outside that

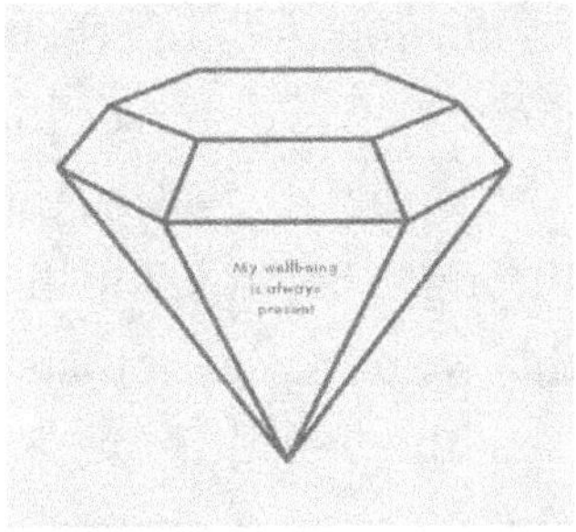

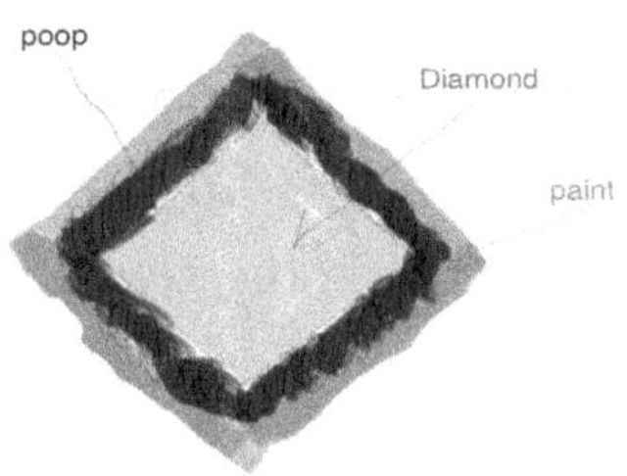

will help or hurt us when we understand this. With the shit BS (belief systems) we accumulate, we are constantly looking outside of ourselves and judging whether we are good or bad. When we don't like our situation or look, we want to hide what we believe to be our true selves, so we put on the paint, faking a diamond. We will discuss this more throughout the book, as this is what will free you from ever feeling less than a diamond, because that is who you truly are. Once you realize this experientially, you will start to free your true self, be comfortable in your own skin, and life will be better than you can ever imagine.

So, let's look at your shit. What is it?

It's the BS (belief systems), limiting beliefs and attitudes, the traumas and experiences that have covered your true self, your diamond, so you cannot see, or even recognize, yourself as the diamond anymore. These are beliefs, so we believe them. They are thoughts we keep thinking with feelings attached that accumulate to an illusion of being the truth in our eyes. We don't see the world with our eyes, we see the world through the filters of all the shit that we have accumulated about how the world is, generalizing almost every situation with

these filters. It's how we take something objective (like a BMW driver), experience subjectively (so maybe a BMW driver cut you off in traffic without signaling and was being a dick), and then make that subjective experience into an objective belief ("All BMW drivers are dicks"). Some of us have just a little shit, and some of us have a truckload. All of us have at least some shit and, let's face it, most of us could fertilize a plantation.

This shit is the stuff that prevents us from living a happy, fulfilling life, free from anxiety and doubt.

Please read that sentence again.

Go on, read it again.

It is what we believe ourselves to be. It is our ego.

We don't like this shit being on show to the public, especially as we believe that this is our true self, who we truly are, our identity, even though it's complete made-up shit!

So, to cover-up, instead of excreting it as we are supposed to, we use some form of shiny paint.

What the heck is the paint? It's all of this and more:

- People-pleasing.

- Arguing.

- Making others wrong just so you look better.

- Blame.

- Gossiping.

- Playing video games.

- Positive affirmations.

- The fake-it-'til-you-make-it walk.

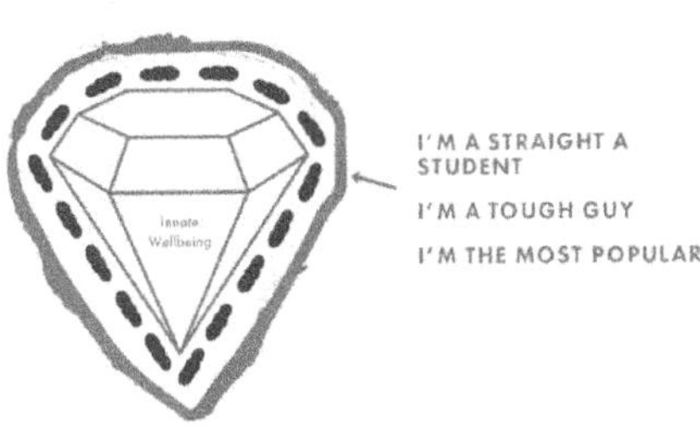

- Using positive thinking to override the negative thinking.

- The straight-A student, the tough guy, the bully.

- The person who must be better than everyone else to prove themselves worthy.

- The "look at me, I'm being funny on Instagram."

- "Wait. Let me take a selfie!"

- Getting as many likes as possible for that cat photo.

- Getting as many relationships as possible, or showing that you have the best relationship, even when it stinks.

- Keeping up with the Joneses.

- The motivational speech, the fancy car or job, the hefty bank account.

- Being constantly busy, and making sure people know it.

- Working harder than anyone else, and making sure people know it.

- Jumping out of airplanes.

- Getting the trophy wife or husband.

- Learning how to win friends and influence people because you are lacking.

- Playing music really loud.

- Deliberately broken mufflers on a Harley-Davidson.

- Name-dropping.

- Hanging out with people mainly because of their prestige and then posting selfies with them on Facebook.

- Facebook.

- Having a house with more square footage than the whole of Switzerland.

- Practicing confidence skills, while still believing in your bullshit belief systems.

- Using alcohol or drugs for Dutch courage.

- Addictions you have unconsciously to escape reality.

- Having to be the life and soul of the party.

- Designer clothes with labels on display.

- Bodybuilding.

- Face "paint."

- Lips that resemble a baboon's ass.

- Flotation devices fitted to the front of our bodies and other "fake bits."

- Any form of trying to compensate for a presumed lack.

- Addictive behavior.

- Labels.

- Some sicknesses that become a reason to not be in the world. Or the loser's limp, like the soccer player that magically jumps up and is cured after the "magic sponge" is used. Not before the ref calls a foul of course.

- Being the victim.

- Belonging to a team, club, or organization and wearing it like a badge of honor to the exclusion of others.

You may have your own versions to add to this list, which can be endless.

Although I poke some fun, please understand that none of this is necessarily wrong (apart from the destructive addictions and habits perhaps). But until you relieve yourself of the shit by realizing the truth of who you really are, they (the actions) will almost always be for the wrong reasons. You use them to hide your "true identity" (in other words the ego that you believe is you), so inevitably they will not and cannot give you the outcome that you are looking for.

Once you remove the shit from your life, you will not need to paint stuff or self-soothe (unless it's fun). It will be a choice, not a need to be validated. You will find the types of paint that suit and compliment your true self, rather than imitate your presumed lack.

We are going to eliminate this shit from your life. Just call me the shit eliminator.

Imagine how your life will be once you take a big dump, and all the shit is eliminated. Imagine breaking the myth of social fear and insecurity once and for all, so that you will not just overcome the fear, not just "feel the fear and do it anyway," not just imagine that you can defeat the fear and find the courage in yourself to overcome this demon, you will realize that there is no fear to conquer. Once this is experienced, like the curtain being pulled back on the Wizard of Oz, the illusion will have lost its power. You unfortunately will accumulate more shit, that's human nature, but you will be able to simply take a dump and carry on.

When we look at the psychology of anxiety, it's like metaphorically trying to move an iceberg, because the illusion, like in the film *The Wizard of Oz*,[7] looks and feels so real. It develops substance and solidifies, like ice. But once we realize that it is an illusion, there is no substance. Like water in its gaseous form, it's extremely easy to move away.

Think of your true self, the diamond, as the sun, and the shit as the clouds. If you didn't know how weather worked, you may be forgiven for thinking that the sun may never shine again on a cloudy day. But realizing that the sun is still shining, just clouded, you can relax, knowing that the clouds will eventually clear. Unless you're in England.

Anxiety tends to be a what-if game, imagining the worst-case scenarios and feeling them in advance whether they will happen or not. Let's change that statement to work for you. What if you could realize in advance that you don't have to suffer? What if you can have a conversation and enjoy it? Or not enjoy it, yet still be fine? You will be fine no matter the situation when you realize that you are not your thinking! You truly are the untarnished, pure diamond.

You never need to clear all the TV channels that you have ever watched in your life to watch the TV station that you want to see now. They may be there in the ether, but they have zero effect on you. Likewise, you do not have to conquer this social block because of all the memories of previous negative experiences. Once you understand the truth, that they are just like those TV channels, you can (if you are crazy and want to) tune into them; that's your choice. But you also have the choice to watch a better channel, and the previous channels have no power over you.

You can free yourself of that shitty social fear, or any fear for that matter.

By understanding where your experience is coming from, you will feel comfortable in your skin regardless of social, or any other, circumstances. You won't feel the need for so much paint. You will still have some, but only because you love it and it enriches your life and improves your skillset, never because you're trying to compensate for a presumed lack.

This book makes life so much simpler than we have been taught. Get ready to watch the thinking of social, or any other fear, disappear. This does not mean that you are going to suddenly become the life and soul of the party if you were not before, but you will feel comfortable in your skin, and people will feel comfortable in your presence. This is the key to a fulfilling life.

As I wrote this, my wife Andi asked if I wanted to meet some people for happy hour, and I said, no! Shock, horror.

Not because of fear though, not because I'm a dick (not in this scenario anyway), but because I tend to be introverted. Meaning: I need to be alone sometimes, or at least be around fewer people, to recharge my batteries occasionally. That doesn't mean that I avoid every social event . . . anymore, (previously I would hide from people, making excuses for why I couldn't attend before they had told me the date or time).What it does mean is that I can simply be myself, not thinking that I need to be someone that I'm not.

With this huge weight off my shoulders, I can enjoy socializing. Why? Not because I learned the ten steps to building charisma, or tips and tricks to get people to like me, but because people like people who are comfortable in their own skin. It gives others unconscious permission to be comfortable, too.

I cannot begin to give justice to how unbelievably life-changing and freeing this will be for you. You won't have to prepare to meet new people, trying to remember the latest strategies and words (like I used to). You won't have to worry whether people will like you. You will just show up and be yourself.

You may ask, "How can I show up as me when I have never experienced who I really am?"

That was my question and concern for most of my life. You possibly have no idea how brilliant you are. But when the shit belief systems are gone, the true light of your diamond shines through.

What you will learn is not a mass of tricks and tactics to get people to like you or to mask the feelings with paint. Those have their place perhaps, but only *after* you have learned to simply be yourself, regardless of circumstances. You are not your shit—you are not your paint either, which is a very poor and tacky imitation of your diamond (your true self).

This is not the usual ten tricks to being social book. This book is going to help you see who you truly are and set your personal thermostat. The rest will fall into place.

Your thermostat, like the thermostat in your home, will be set at the correct temperature for you to live your best life, your way. It will give you a deep understanding of what causes anxiety and how to stop it before it starts, allowing you to be comfortable in your own skin.

You will learn how to play the warmer, colder game in your life and how to tap into your inner GPS, tapping into your innate wisdom.

You will become an expert decision maker, learning how to use all three of your brains. Yeah, I said it, there are three. You will have the most amazing relationships by knowing why we are all living in separate realities, and what everyone wants.

Before you move on to chapter one, ask yourself these questions:

1. What would you love to gain from reading this book?

2. What will having that true self-confidence do for you?

If you would like to share your answers, please join the Facebook group kickthesh#toutof, or email me personally at lee.vallely@ yahoo.com

Now a very simple, yet possibly the most important, exercise:

Place the tongue on the roof of the mouth. Without realizing we tend to have constant chatter, so by placing the tongue on the roof of the mouth, among many other benefits, helps to lessen the chatter automatically because we actually enact the words unconsciously.

Breathe in and out through your nose, at your own pace, for the rest of your life.

When do you stop? When you cannot breathe through your nose. So, if you have a cold, it may be difficult, or when you are speaking, of course. If you are working out, try to breathe through your nose as much as you can. Obviously, if it's a heavy workout then it's going to be difficult. But please, do the best you can.

So just becoming a nose breather will help to start to break the illusion of anxiety. When we feel anxious, we tend to breathe through the mouth, trying to get as much oxygen into the body as we can, as the fight or flight response has been activated. Unwittingly, the fight or flight response can also be activated simply by mouth breathing.

When you breathe through the nose, you activate the parasympathetic nervous system, sometimes called your rest and digest state. This is, among many other things, a way to help your body and mind stay in a calm state, regardless of circumstances.

CHAPTER I

Kick The Shit Out of Your Thinking: Don't Think, Feel

"It's like a finger pointing away to the moon.
Don't concentrate on the finger or you
will miss all that heavenly glory."[8]

BRUCE LEE

For decades, in fact, for almost my entire intellectual life, I have been focusing on, learning, and trying every strategy, exercise, and concept I could find, including learning from Bob Proctor (narrator of *The Secret)*, motivational guru Tony Robbins, and Richard Bandler, the cofounder of Neuro Linguistic Programming (NLP). I searched for anything I could find to get rid of the bullshit belief systems that I had created. I have great respect for all these teachings, but for me there was just one fundamental flaw in common with all of these theories, which once realized can make these either work incredibly better, or become totally unnecessary.

Neuro Linguistic Programming (NLP)[5] is a study of excellence intended to program your mind into getting the results you want and replacing the programs that don't serve you. NLP deciphers what works for you by using the language of the mind to learn strategies on changing habits, beliefs, values, and anything that is not of service to you and replaces it with what will work, with the emphasis, for me, on being comfortable, if not amazing, socially.

Did it work? Well, I would say that sometimes it did by default—unfortunately never permanently. It covered over my insecurities rather than eliminating them; painting over the shit which I now realize are illusions.

One major tactic I learned was focusing on the other person or people rather than on myself. Whether I was teaching a class, giving a speech, or just conversing with someone, being "them" focused sometimes helped me get out of my head, as the emphasis was on their performance, not mine. Well, that is until they either dried up, felt like I was interrogating them, or they turned the tables and started asking me "rude" questions about my personal life—how very dare they!?—even though the questions were the identical questions I was asking them.

There may have been a flaw in my approach. I needed to find my being.

I realized that I was afraid of being myself.

I was trying to be them, rather than simply being myself, without understanding that I already had everything that I needed. You don't have to remind yourself to like something if you already like it. You don't have to remind yourself not to order steak when you're a vegan or greens if you are a carnivore.

This fundamental change is what set me free. The diamond (your true self) doesn't have a communication problem. Or any problem, for that matter. It's the illusionary shit that makes you believe that you are lacking in any way.

I was taught this simple change of thinking in my experience, which I am teaching you in this book, although I've worded it somewhat differently. I had heard about this many times before but didn't really appreciate its power to truly impact one's life when it's put into practice, or, more accurately, experienced as true. I thought I was already living this way, but boy was I wrong.

The good news for you is that once you get it, you get it.

Before I "got it," I was fighting these "evil" limiting beliefs and thoughts.

Now, I'm merely reminding myself that it is just a movie, a dream; albeit a very persistent one.

Simple, huh? Yeah, but not so easy when you have been believing this other (shit) way of thinking your whole life.

Have you ever used virtual reality goggles? It's not just a movie passing in front of your eyes; you're in the movie. I went to a place called Alton Towers in England as a kid, which is like the English version of Disney World. They had this dome cinema there. They'd project the movie on the inside of the dome, so you were surrounded by the film and you really felt like you were in the movie. I could have sworn that the ground and walls were moving, but it was all in my mind. I remember when they played a film of a rollercoaster, I almost threw up, but tried to look cool in front of my friends, so I pretended it didn't faze me. Unfortunately, I failed miserably when they showed a ski slope movie and I fell onto my friend.

As real as that seemed, it's not even close to how realistic our thinking is. It looks, smells, tastes, sounds, and feels 100 percent authentic. In fact, it's the only "reality" that we have ever experienced. But as we realize the truth, that we are not, let's say, afraid of social situations but rather of a "movie" playing in our minds of a future social event, we gradually let that fear subside.

NLP was so close to the truth (in my opinion), which is why it took centuries . . . okay decades, for me to see this for myself. Because to me, it looked like they were saying the same thing.

NLP was stating (in my opinion) that we make up everything, so if we're going to make shit up, why not make up good shit that serves us? It made perfect sense to me and sounds just like the "it's a movie" idea. Except that it is still encouraging us to do something about "it," yet the "it" doesn't exist. By doing something about "it," you are accepting the problem as actually existing; as being 100 percent real. You are still in the illusion of being broken.

NLP seemed to me to be the way to freedom and happiness. So why, in 2007, was I in Palm Springs, California, in the fetal position, hysterically crying on a hotel bathroom floor?

I was a leader for a Tony Robbins seminar[9] and was, along with my colleague, responsible for looking after about sixty of the 2,000 participants in the seminar. This was a huge deal for me. I wasn't just taking part and learning from, in my opinion, one of the best in the business—I was a representative. I knew my stuff; I had it together. So how could the 'got it all together' Lee Vallely be on the hotel bathroom floor hysterically crying his eyes out?

I felt completely lost. I had almost lost my voice at that point from working in the freezing arctic, zero-degree temperature of the air-conditioned rooms, contracting some flu bug perhaps (this was pre-Covid) and had experienced a lack of sleep since in those days, we would start the day at around 7:00 a.m., an hour before the participants arrived, and not leaving until 2:00 a.m. most nights. It's more relaxed now, but that's how it was back then. So many emotions were at play.

But the main reason I, the mighty leader man, who, being typically English "doesn't do emotions," was hysterically crying was because I felt like I had reached the end of the trail. I believed that I had truly learned all I could to fix myself. I was a leader for Tony Robbins, for crying out loud! There was nowhere else to go, nothing else to learn, no one else to turn to, yet I was still broken.

I felt just like I did in my early days as a kid, like I was a complete fraud. Maybe they were right; maybe I was a piece of shit, a nothing. How could I be there for these people (who really did rely on us leaders to guide them on their journey through the seminar) when I couldn't fix myself? I was miserable, almost suicidal, and I felt terrified and alone. I felt that the stuff they taught, which I supposedly believed in and was preaching, didn't work—not for me anyway.

Of course, then it was showtime, so eventually, I realized that I needed to pull myself together and fake it till I made it by putting a smile on my face and pretending that everything was wonderful.

Isn't it incredible how we can do that? One minute I'm having a psychological breakdown, and the next I'm putting on my best shirt to look good while changing lives for the better. Amazingly, I could walk on stage and speak to thousands of people without hesitation yet was terrified of having a conversation with anyone in the crowd.

Your King Lear Is Shit

I love the analogy that the amazing Rupert Spira, author of many fabulous books, including *The Nature of Consciousness*,[10] uses. He says to imagine yourself as John/Jane Smith (there's no gender at the spiritual level) playing the part of King Lear in this movie called Life. (I personally would have liked to have thought of myself as playing 007, but still.) Our persona, our ego, our shit, and our paint are King Lear (James Bond), yet we unconsciously buy in to the idea that we are this fictitious character. Even though we have made up everything about King Lear through parents, teachers, guardians, bullies, and peers, molding our values and beliefs, it's still not us that has been molded; it's the part of us acting as King Lear (ego). As soon as we realize that we are simply playing a part and are not really King Lear, we no longer need to make up anything or improve anything to do with this character. King Lear/Lee Vallely/007/insert your name is merely a character created by all the bullshit beliefs that have made a personality that we think is ourselves. This is not true. It is an illusion that covers our true selves, our diamond. NLP might sway you to make up new shit, which can help temporarily, but that's simply adding to the pile. When you realize the truth, you can still play the game, though now with a diamond authenticity.

You cannot fix an illusion; you can, however, realize that it doesn't exist. It feels very real for all of us. King Lear is the only person we have ever experienced; it's like we've only been one character in a sitcom or drama our entire lives. Though if King Lear doesn't exist, why would we need to fix anything about him/her/them? No wonder I was driving myself crazy, trying to fix an illusory problem in myself, creating a feeling of anxiety in the process.

This is so simple when you step out of the cinedome, yet it is almost impossible to see while you're trapped in it. Even top actors can get sucked into the role that they are playing, because they are feeling and experiencing how their fictitious character, in their mind, would feel, react, judge, and carry themselves. Having the upbringing, experiences, etc., in their lives, they feel as if they were real. Imagine playing that character for your entire life! That's exactly what you've been doing.

I heard of a top actor who had a ritual of mentally hanging their ego on a hangar in their dressing room so that they could play the characters but never get affected by them. It's only our ego that can be affected because this personality *is* our ego. The true self, the diamond, is intact, unaffected by what life throws at us.

Positive Thinking Is Just More Shit and Paint

Most people have heard of, and possibly tried to, change their mind, their habits of thinking, and their limiting thought patterns, trying to catch each thought and stop thinking that way, then try to think the opposite. It's exhausting! Also, impossible! You cannot change a thought once it has been thought. That's like trying to change a chair back into a tree. Too late. We then try to create positive thoughts to counteract the negative thoughts, but now we have overloaded our minds with double the number of thoughts.

Imagine your mind like a snow globe, and your thoughts are the snow. If your mind is filled with negative thoughts and then you add the same number of positive thoughts (more snow), how muddled do you think your mind is going to be? But imagine if those negative thoughts in your mind were allowed to settle down? A clear mind is inevitable, giving clear thought. Trying to force positive thinking is painting a poor simulation of clear thought. Our innate well-being is naturally positive. So, fresh thinking is positive without our intervention.

There's no struggle to positive thinking, as we've innocently been led to believe; it is our natural ability. Like the body naturally heals a cut, the mind naturally flows positive thoughts. Our mind will flow positive thoughts without us trying to conjure them up. In fact, the thoughts are better than we could conjure up because they are clear and untarnished, whereas whatever we can muster up from our personal mind will be a memory or repeat of something in the past.

So how do we catch all these thoughts and settle them down?

It's been said that we think around 70,000 thoughts per day,[11] with 80 percent, if not all sometimes, being recycled thoughts. That's way too many to try to keep track of. But we live in the "feeling" of our thinking.

We don't have to find the "snow" (thought, belief, circumstance; shit) that's causing the problem, we will just get lost in even more snow. But if we notice our feelings, we can tell whether we have "stinking thinking" or not. What if we had no judgments about our feelings?

If you have anxious feelings, you don't need a psychology degree to figure out that you may be having anxious thoughts. Contrary to popular belief, you don't have to seek those thoughts out, get them on the *analyst* chair, and examine every damn detail. Just noticing the feeling has already created awareness of what you're thinking.

Unfortunately, we humans have this habit of judging the heck out of our feelings. We unwittingly look for the reason we're feeling this way and, consequently, we find something—anything—that fits the bill. If you want to find a reason to feel anxious, regardless of how badly, or well, your life is going, do you think you could?

I think so too. In fact, I would be so bold as to say, I know so.

It's "normal" to look outside of yourself for the answer to what's happening inside of you. Your feelings are like a human barometer, not for your surroundings or your circumstances, but for your thinking.

The cause is not the thought or situation that created the feeling, the cause is the judgment.

Imagine if you just noticed the feeling without the judgment? Without seeking the culprit?

Here's the question: how would you know whether that feeling was good or bad?

It's a tough one I know, because it's messing with your entire existence. This is not easy to grasp, but it makes sense, right? If there's no judgment, then there's no way of experiencing a good or bad feeling. It's merely a feeling.

You might say (because I did at this point), "If there's no good or bad feelings except through judgment, does that mean I will be stuck with the feelings I have?"

Yes and no.

I appreciate that you may want to slap me right now, but please stay with me as you are about to transform your life for the better.

Kick the Shit Out of Your Fears

When I was using NLP, I was great at curing phobias. In fact, I had a 100 percent success rate in England. (I say in England because I did a phobia cure in the United States with a therapist, in front of a group of therapists, and it didn't go well, to say the least. The therapists attacked me so badly that I got into my head and doubted something I could normally do in my sleep. I now have a phobia of therapists.) So, if I had a 100 percent success rate, why the heck wasn't I the most famous guy in the UK?

Because people were afraid to come to me. Not because they doubted my abilities, but because they were afraid to face their fears, which were phobic fears, in other words, *irrational*. They would rather live with the phobia than go through the most terrifying experience that they could possibly imagine, which was to face the phobia. I guess I needed better marketing skills, because the truth is that you never need to face your fears—they don't exist, at least as we have imagined them. This is why phobias are "irrational" fears.

In my opinion, social anxiety tends to be fearing the potential of being rejected, embarrassed, judged, or humiliated in some way. Then accumulating judgments on every word said and action that you took. Is it any wonder you fear social interactions with this going on in your head? You set yourself up to fail, then berate yourself for every little mistake, even when no one else would have even noticed it as such. This was my life for decades.

What you think of as fear most often is an imaginary state. Remember that our *natural* feelings are that of innate well-being.

So, when left alone, you naturally return to a "positive" state. When you label your feelings, you are keeping them active, even if you are not physically doing anything to activate them. This is thought to be normal.

It is pointless to pretend that we are feeling good when we have labeled the feelings as bad. As a result of the feeling, certain anxiety-inducing chemicals have been released in the body and take a little time to leave the bloodstream. Being aware of this, however, speeds up that process, as the change in perception naturally changes the chemicals being released, from anxiety-inducing to neutral, allowing a calm mindset and, after some initial practice, the feeling defaults to our innate well-being, the positive feeling of peace, happiness, joy, contentment, and love.

When we simply accept the feelings without judgment, that simple act eventually neutralizes, or positivizes, the feelings (I think I made a word).

Some people ask me, "What if the negative feelings are trying to tell me something?" That stumped me for a while because there are times in my life when I had a negative gut feeling about something and it was correct—many times, in fact. I now realize that it was the labeling that led me to believe that the "negative" feelings were warning me, when it was simply my inner GPS giving a signal that I was off course, then I attached judgmental feelings, believing that it was the negative feelings guiding me, putting two things together and making a false assumption. Hey, even a clock that has stopped shows the right time twice a day. Correlation is not necessarily truth.

Innate wisdom does not mean you're floating on cloud nine, not knowing your ass from your elbow. It means you're tuned in, tapped in, and turned on. You are in the zone, as the athletes call it. In the flow. Whatever you want to call it, it's good shit, I mean diamond.

Remember the warmer or colder game? Just like the warmer or colder game, you know in your body if it's metaphorically warmer or colder and readjust, no negative judgments or stories necessary.

Would you agree that you are more likely to deal with a situation better when you have a clear mind rather than in a frantic, stressed, negative state? We are, at the very least, more likely to make better decisions about any situation in innate well-being than we are in any other state. When you're in a cloudy state, you cannot see solutions, only problems. When you're in a clear state—in the zone—you cannot see problems, only solutions.

Even pure fear, in its true form, can put us into the innate wisdom state. Most people mistake pure fear for worry, anxiety, or stress. These states are caused by overthinking thoughts that project either future catastrophes or negative past events. This is not pure fear.

Pure fear is experienced in the present moment, and it creates clarity of mind. Senses are heightened. Some people in the military and similar jobs have even claimed that time seems to slow down in the face of pure fear. Pure fear is only in the present. This is describing the same feelings as being in the flow or zone. Doesn't it make sense that if the body is in imminent danger, the mind would become clear, not foggy?

I experienced a scary example of this. I was walking along the Intracoastal Waterway where a lot of homes alongside it have dogs. As I passed one house that had a long driveway, two huge Rottweilers came running out and headed toward me, growling but not barking.

I absolutely love dogs and am used to having dogs run and bark at me, so normally this would be no big deal. But this was different; these dogs were coming toward me like predators ready to take down their prey.

My initial feeling was terror. They were not warning me, they were coming for me. Intuitively, unconsciously I guess, I switched to a zone-like state. It was instantaneous.

I only realize this now while looking back. It's almost like it happened in slow motion because I recall every detail. It felt like the noisy, anxious me was pushed aside willingly, while the "real" me took over. I didn't feel anything except a clear knowing. Not like an "aha!" type of knowing, but a deep knowing beyond anything I can describe.

It sounds crazy, I know. It's so hard to describe the feeling, and it was only seconds in duration.

I suddenly reached out my hand (which, by the way, is the worst thing to do to a scary Rottweiler normally), and purposefully brushed the alpha dogs back, that's how close they were to me by this time. The dogs looked confused; they didn't go all friendly and acknowledge me, as a normal encounter with a dog might happen. They loudly growled some more, looking me in the eyes, almost like they were checking my authenticity, then turned around and went back into their garden.

It was one of those "you had to be there" moments, because I'm sure if I were reading this, I would think it was just in the writer's mind. Maybe it was, but the way they reacted was not normal, I promise you. My actions were instinctual and clear, like something was guiding me, yet wasn't separate from me.

I don't recommend that you try this out for yourself, but I do want you to know that this power is in you too, especially when you need it most. It's this clarity of mind that is your natural state. We've covered it over with this shit; so much so that it doesn't feel "normal."

A lot of people would say that their natural state is worry and anxiety, or at least bordering more on the negative side. But we sometimes mistake "normal" for "natural." *Normal* is our learned, intellectual, and survivalist behavior that has developed to keep us safe. In other words, our shit in the form of ego. *Natural* is our pure state, without contamination from outside influences, in other words, our diamond or true self.

Can you imagine living in this natural state every moment of your entire life? Well, you can't. Let me explain.

It's not impossible to live in this state permanently, I'm sure as heck working on it. However, as many will point out, we live in the "real world." Now, as much as I would question whether you have ever really lived in the "real world," for fear of being that guy, let's just agree that we are drawn into the illusionary shit constantly. Apart from fleeting moments of clarity, this shit is all we know.

Therefore people (me included, in the not-so-distant past) will refer to it as the "real world." The illusion is so strong because you've lived in this ego illusion your entire intellectual life. You have only ever experienced an interpretation of the outside world by your senses and filtered through your BS, your belief systems that were created when you were five years old or so. You have never seen a tree, only your ego bullshit belief interpretation of a tree.

You don't have to learn to have self-esteem; you have self-esteem. You don't have to find happiness or learn to be comfortable in your skin; you are comfortable, you are the diamond experiencing an illusion of limitations (ego).

George Pransky, a brilliant mentor and author of *The Relationship Handbook*,[12] was once asked by a student, "So you are telling me that everything I've ever thought to be real is just a mirage?!"

And George said, "Well, it is a real mirage."

That may take some time to sink in. It did for me when I first heard it. Take a breath. Read it again.

You are experiencing an interpretation, not pure reality. That understanding can make the transition easier, albeit frustrating at first.

Just remember that, like the mirage, there's something there. In the case of the mirage, there's a trick of the light, the heat, and the sand so you think you see water. The experience itself is real but the content of the experience is the mirage. There are no unreal experiences, just unreal situations or circumstances. Like processed food, we are living in a self-processed world.

Please just take another deep breath.

Crazy! Say What?

- Trying to exchange one belief for another is painting over the illusionary shit. Let's eliminate the shit and get back to our innate well-being, our diamond, by realizing the truth.

- Our "normal" state is distorted by our shit filters, so we almost never actually experience reality, we experience a refined, filtered, tainted version of reality, like a mirage. When we can take away the veil of shit and paint (alias our ego), we experience reality in our "natural" state, which is clear, untainted, tapped into the flow or the zone. It's good shit (okay not any shit really, it's the diamond, but good shit sounded better).

- When we realize that we are not the character we are playing in the game of life, we can allow our true selves to shine through. King Lear/James Bond/ego is not really broken because it's only a fictitious character. Give yourself a break though, you have only ever known yourself as this character. It may take a while to sink in. You will be exposed to this repetitively throughout the reading of this book.

- We don't experience pure fear very often, if ever. We experience worry and/or anxiety. A feeling of worry or anxiety is drifting into the thinking of the future or dwelling on the past. Pure fear is totally present in the now and is clear. It can be relied upon when we need it.

- Most people with phobias would, understandably, rather stay with the phobia than face their fears. You don't have to face your fears, you simply must realize that they are only an illusion, a mirage, albeit a very "real" feeling one. The experience of anxiety is a real experience; the content is the mirage.

- Our natural state is from our diamond, or rather, we are the diamond; the shit (ego) and paint is the mirage.

- Being your natural self takes no energy. A dog spends no energy being a dog, yet we spend enormous energy trying to be this made-up character rather than simply being our perfect selves. Once this is realized, any social anxiety or any fear will be a thing of the past. You may need to take a dump to just eliminate the shit occasionally.

Exercise:

BREATHE.

Breathe in through the nose, and as you do imagine the word "let," or even say it in your mind. Then breathe out, preferably through the nose, as you say or imagine the word "go."

I would suggest that you do this first thing in the morning to start the day without any baggage, then again whenever you remember to. Don't get into a full anxiety state then try this because you need to build the psychological muscle of being able to let go. If you are in an anxious state, then cup your hands and breathe in and out through them, through the nose as much as possible, but again don't wait for an attack. Practice this over and over and eventually you won't have to deal with anxiety.

Remember when you tasted your first beer, or whiskey, or any alcoholic drink. If you have never drank, then choose something similar.

Did you think it tasted delicious? Admittedly, the food and drink industry are smart, so have made some pop alcoholic drinks taste good, but most people will agree that it was disgusting. Yet we convince ourselves to like it through our social conditioning. I remember my first Guinness. OMG it was disgusting, but I taught myself to love it, because that's what all the cool kids drank (in England anyway).

If you ever smoked or tried a cigarette, remember that first drag? I remember my cousin getting me to collect and take all the empty bottles to the store that gave us five pence per bottle. I wanted to buy sweets, but my cousin insisted we get cigarettes. They did not taste anywhere near as good as sweets, but I wanted to impress my cousin and pretended to like them, almost coughing out a lung in the process. The list can go on, like with coffee; imagine tasting it for the first time without cream or sugar.

This will give you an insight into how we can brainwash ourselves into believing, over time and social conditioning, that something is different than what our first impression may have been.

If these examples do not work for you then come up with one of your own. It's simply to open us up to the awareness that we create filters for what we perceive as reality. This is the "real" mirage. And please, do this. We know these things intellectually, but it's only experientially that we make a change.

Sit on a chair, how does that feel? Now imagine that this chair has been in your family for generations, your great grandfather used to sit in that very chair and even further back. Now imagine that it is coated with asbestos and is toxic to you and the environment. Then imagine it to be blessed by a very spiritual guru who meditated on this chair for decades.

Again, create your own examples, but see how your interpretation of that chair changes with every example. This is obvious intellectually, but the change comes from experience, so please experience this for yourself. This is an exercise, not just a sentence with words in it.

Imagine the top half of your head like a snow globe. Imagine all that snow as thoughts in your mind.

Just like the snow globe, rather than adding to it, allow it (your head) to simply relax, and allow all that snow (thoughts) to settle down, allowing pure thought to come through. Again, practice this daily and not when there is an emergency, because you want to get good at this in advance. Make it a little ritual, like first thing when you wake up and last thing at night, plus anytime in the day when you remember. Then it will become habitual.

CHAPTER 2

Kick the Shit Out of Your Beliefs: Set Your Thermostat Not Your Thermometer

"If we learned to walk and talk the way we learned to read and write, everyone would limp and stutter."[13]

MARK TWAIN

I enjoy meeting new, as well as familiar, people . . . occasionally. This was sooooo not the case in my previous life. Before this understanding of the diamond and where our experiences are coming from (this being the understatement of the millennium), I dreaded going to any social events, even if I knew a few people . . . hey, even if I knew everyone! The best news ever was when an event was canceled. I would be that guy who would be ready with an excuse for why I couldn't go to an event before they even told me what the event was, or what date it was on. Got caught out with that one a few times, too.

Now I'm content within myself. I'm still not a socialite, though now I make my decision of whether to attend an event or not based on what I want rather than from fear (shit), so I say yes more often and, most of the time, enjoy myself. I cannot tell you that I feel comfortable in every situation, meeting, or event, because that wouldn't be truthful, but I *can* tell you that I feel comfortable within and about myself at every event. This may not seem that big of a deal to some people, but for me it was, and is, life-changing.

Why am I telling you this? Why wouldn't I? It's cool.

The other reason is that, even though in the past I learned plenty of strategies and techniques that I thought would finally get me to feeling comfortable in social situations, they didn't work permanently—for me, that is. Why? Because my thermostat kicked in.

Imagine you are in a room where the thermostat is set at sixty-eight degrees. Then someone comes into the room, leaving the door open and letting the cold in. Immediately the heaters kick in and go to work to force that temperature up to, or slightly over, the sixty-eight degrees, it overcompensates so that eventually, it evens out again to sixty-eight degrees. I live in South Florida. So, if someone opened the door here the temperature would probably shoot up. So, the air conditioners would kick in and freeze the place until it balanced out and got back down to just below sixty-eight degrees again.

It's like diets. People say that diets don't work, but almost all do work (temporarily). There's just one problem: most people don't stick to them. In fact, 98 percent of people who go on a diet statistically fail.

The people who didn't get results trying to follow the diet or, like me, trying to learn the techniques to be a social stud, didn't change the inner thermostat to accommodate this change. They were more like thermometers, living their lives and adjusting their moods based on the outside temperature (situation, circumstance, thoughts), instead of controlling that temperature internally (thermostat). When you want to make a change in your life, but your thermostat is still stuck in your previous way of thinking, you are in a constant battle with yourself, you are incongruent, and you are going to lose almost every time.

If your inner thermostat was where you wanted it to be—a certain weight, financial situation, or comfort level in social situations—you wouldn't need a book, diet, or anything else to get you there, because nothing would stop you from getting and staying there. If it's not, even if by sheer willpower you force yourself to the weight, social level, or financial success, nothing will help you stay there. If you think willpower will get you through, try holding your breath and use willpower to override the body, forcing you to let go of that breath. You may even get into the *Guinness Book of Records* for the time that you held it, but the body (almost) always wins, and will probably make you pass out so that you're horizontal and start breathing again.

What if your thermostat was set to 188 pounds, and you wanted to be at 172? So, you go on a diet and lose ten pounds. But then the body heaters kick in and put chemicals in your system to make you hungry AF. You can't help yourself, you must eat, the craving is almost as powerful as the need to breathe, and before you know it, you're not only back ten pounds but even a pound or six more as the thermostat resets itself.

What if you, like me, try a few strategies and get tips and tricks to be the life and soul of the party? You go into unknown territory armed with new tricks to try out and get some great results. You then take it to the next level and begin saying yes to invites and start to feel better about socializing, like you've finally broken free. Then the air conditioners kick in and create slip-ups, thoughts, and feelings to sabotage situations, make you feel like an ass, and bring you back to being "the awkward socializer" that your thermostat is programmed to make you be. In fact, you are overcompensating, and you feel even more battle-shy than before as the thermostat regulates itself.

It's imperative that we understand that it is not in the *doing* that we will be comfortable with ourselves in social, or any, situations. The setting of your thermostat is not in the doing, it is in the being, beyond even the identity level. Beyond the shit beliefs that hold our thermostat in place (the ego). Then you will feel what the right actions to take are.

I'm sure you have heard this many times before, as had I. I believed that the strategies were teaching me to overcome this obstacle so that I would "be the change." Hence the lying on the bathroom floor, hysterically crying incident that I mentioned earlier. I could not understand why the strategies were not working, when I was doing them religiously every day.

Generally, when we look at changing our being, we look at our values, beliefs, and habits. After all, that's what's creating the problem, as this is the shit covering our diamond. This is what I did for decades, and I was great at it, but it didn't work for me; not permanently anyway. The damn air conditioners would kick in and bring me back to "where I belong." I was unwittingly trying to cover the shit with paint.

I remember watching a YouTube video of a guy who taught PUA. If you are not familiar with the term (I had to look it up) it's a "pickup artist." As in showing people how to pick up a date.

This guy taught his group exactly what to say to get the results. They show a video of one of the guys trying to connect with a girl and failing miserably. The words were perfect, he just wasn't comfortable saying them, so he appeared a little creepy. He was changing his temperature by saying the right words, but his thermostat was causing his energy to be incongruent, and the AC kicked in (to be fair, if I knew a secret camera was on me, I would be nervous, too).

The instructor then went into the same club, and even the same group of ladies, saying the same thing! Exactly the same words. They loved him and hung out all night with him. This blew my mind in one sense but confirms the thermostat perfectly. To the instructor's credit he addressed this problem really well.

The world is simply a mirror of our thoughts. The world reflects our inner self (not our inner being, that's perfect, we are talking about the self that you believe is you, your ego self). So, just like when you look in a real mirror, you wouldn't try to change the mirror if you didn't like how your hair looked . . . would you? I hope not anyway. You would fix what is being reflected. Most of us are trying to change not who we are, but who we are playing. John Smith (there's no gender at our true essence remember) doesn't need to fix King Lear/007. King Lear is the reflection in this metaphor. John Smith simply realizes it is merely a reflection or an act.

Trust me, I understand that this is a lot to process. But with each chapter the truth begins to unfold, and you will find your thermostat changing even before you have finished reading this book.

But wait, don't order yet, there's more than just the thermostat changing in social situations. You will find your whole life thermostat changing for the better, forever.

You cannot unsee the truth once you have seen it. The sun is always there, even when it is cloudy. You may not see it, but when you know the truth, you know the sun is something you can rely on and that eventually it will shine through again because it was always shining, even in England.

I had a revelation recently of my life as a metaphor. After all, what's a meta . . . for? Not funny? Okay moving on . . .

I've often heard and told the story of a caterpillar going into a chrysalis. A man is watching the caterpillar as it reaches this transformational stage until finally, the almost-fully formed butterfly sticks its head out. It seems to struggle to free itself. A long time passes, and the future butterfly is still really straining and struggling. Thinking he's helping, the man cuts the cocoon and sets the butterfly free, not realizing that in the struggle to free itself, the butterfly was strengthening, squeezing, and cleaning the fluid from its wings. So, without that struggle, the butterfly ends up deformed with swollen wings and never flies.

This is a great metaphor for our own struggles in life as well as our responsibility to help, but not interfere with, other people's struggles.

The metaphor for myself was slightly different, though all those parts to it were still relevant. I realized that I had lived my life as a caterpillar. No, I didn't have loads of hairy legs, and I'm not a fan of lettuce. But I felt like I couldn't fly, as in be successful, or be free from social awkwardness.

I did have an insatiable appetite for knowledge (the metaphorical lettuce or whatever). Particularly, I wanted information on how to fix myself, on self-help and personal growth, on how to be socially accepted, and on how to break free of shyness and social anxiety, which I had struggled with my entire intellectual life. This is like the caterpillar on a feeding frenzy, unwittingly preparing for the transformation. I got better at being in the world and feeling more comfortable and more confident—though never comfortable enough to break the shackles of anxiety and habits that were not serving me. In other words, I hadn't changed my thermostat.

Then, as I learned more and more about the understanding of the diamond and not the shit being the true self, I withdrew even more from the outside world—almost living my entire existence at home. This was the opposite of what I was trying to convince myself to do. The global pandemic gave me an excuse to withdraw even more—if that were possible. I didn't go into a shop or grocery store for about a year because Mr. Stubborn (aka me) didn't like to be forced to wear a mask. Of course, now I understand why masks were necessary, but at the time I thought it was over the top. So, my poor wife, Andi, went instead.

Then, amazingly, I ended up getting COVID-19. I was the one person who was most unlikely to get it, as I rarely left my house. I was bedridden and in total lockdown, confined to my bedroom for well over a week, and didn't see anyone or go anywhere for four weeks, just to be safe for others. While in my pity pot, I read *The Artist's Way* by Julia Cameron,[14] a great book from the nineties that really opened my eyes to creativity. The one exercise I practiced that deeply resonated with me, though it scared me to death, was to have a week without any books, TV, YouTube, social media, or anything that could influence my thinking in any way. The idea is to make room for your own thoughts to come through. What a concept!

You might read this and think, *okay, it's a little daunting maybe, but not that terrible, and it's only for a week.* Not so for me. I don't think I have ever gone an entire week, certainly in my adult life, without reading, or at the very least listening to something nonfiction. What was I supposed to do to occupy myself?! The thought of this terrified me, but for some reason, I felt compelled to do it. I hadn't even finished the book yet. And I couldn't anyway, as I had to stop reading for a week.

I cannot begin to tell you how many revelations, insights, and aha moments I had while in this situation of no distractions. I realized that I had never, to my knowledge, had thought for myself! I'm sure maybe some of my thoughts got through, but I doubt whether I had experienced almost any unprocessed, untainted, pure thoughts that came from my wisdom alone.

I understood the difference between a philosopher, which is what I was being in a sense, and a theosopher. I had never even investigated the idea of theosophy, mainly because I thought this meant biblical studies and, in my ignorance, I thought that this was ignorant.

I believed theosophy only studied religion and therefore was biased. I now realize, or at least my translation is, that theosophy is thinking for the self in spiritual terms, so religion at its source, in its true sense. Above the maze, the matrix of the physical, if you like. It's bringing out your own wisdom, not listening to others, and deciding whether to agree. Not blindly sharing others' ideas and philosophies and living by them. Not even gaining knowledge and creating your own ideas from it as I did, and presuming I was extremely, intellectually aware and wise . . . or so I thought.

It was pure, unadulterated, untainted, unblemished wisdom coming through as fresh thinking. OMG!

This, I appreciate, will not necessarily strike you the way it did for me. That's how insights work, it seems. But for me, it was like a bomb went off in my head. I had never even once questioned the constant learning, reading, and living by, to my illusion, the expert opinions of people much better qualified than myself. In my mind, I was broken and not worthy, so why the heck would I trust anything I thought of myself? That was ludicrous, in my mind.

This insight made the metaphor of the caterpillar feel like it was the story of my life.

I realized that I was in the cocoon right then, and the old beliefs, patterns, and barriers were starting to dissolve into the soup of that cocoon. My thermostat was changing.

I realized that baby steps are vitally important (when I say "realized," I am talking about experientially, not just intellectually). There are exceptions, of course, where people, me included, have had insights that seem to create a transformation that may be bypassed a thousand steps or two. But this is the exception, not the rule, and won't necessarily take you all the way. For the most part, baby steps of repetition and patience were most definitely virtues. They were for me anyway.

I want to stress that I already knew this intellectually but didn't *realize* it experientially. The trouble was that I thought that I did know it, however, and that's sometimes the trap of an intellectual understanding. When we stop rushing to get to the next level and just allow what we have experienced to percolate, wisdom, like an inner GPS, lets us know when we're ready to step up. That would be instantaneous, but for our thinking—our interference.

I realized that I was in my cocoon and had been for some time. I saw how I was hiding from the world and living life through books, audio, videos, etc.

Another astonishing revelation for me was that I was living socially through TV! I was not an avid TV watcher, although I did grow up with the TV almost constantly on as a kid. Without realizing it (I sort of knew intellectually), the TV had become my crutch, my comfort zone. When I did go out socially, even if it was a fun night, I would come home and watch TV as a reward for having to go through "such trauma." In fact, it was my reward for most things. This I understood, but the big realization was that I was using TV as my safe socializing.

Have you ever watched a movie star or presenter and felt like you knew them? Like if they passed you on the street, you would recognize each other. I know you wouldn't believe that . . . would you? But subconsciously, it sometimes seems like it.

I did a lot of speaking, live broadcasts, and interviews—and it's so funny the number of times people would come up to me and start a conversation, telling me they felt like they knew me because they had watched my videos, etc. It was both flattering and fascinating. (Never been asked for my autograph though, unfortunately.)

I realized that, like those people who had watched me, the sitcoms and the movies I was watching were indirectly feeding my social needs. I felt like I was interacting with the characters; like we were friends.

Please don't phone the hospital to put me away. I knew intellectually that this was not true, it was just a subconscious feeling, and I never realized how deep this feeling was. This was satiating, so I never felt the need to go through the "trauma" of really socializing.

When I stopped defaulting to the TV however, I found myself going for walks on "the Ave," as we Delray Beach locals call it. I realized that all that time I thought was wasted on small talk when I could have been learning something new was, in fact, the best way for me to put what I had learned about being in the world with others into practice. To experience rather than intellectualize and philosophize.

It sounds so obvious as I write it down, but I didn't see it in myself before. Have you ever been guilty of this?

Once realized though, change happened effortlessly, like my thermostat was moving by itself. The baby steps were put into place (mainly because I wasn't doing much else, so may as well go to the meeting or the art exhibition, etc.). This was dissolving my kryptonite to allow my thermostat to reset, in a sense.

To say I was not comfortable socially would be the understatement of the millennium; in fact, two millennia. The idea of going to a networking event felt like going for a midnight swim in shark-infested waters with a bloody fish tied around my neck. In fact, I may have opted for that instead, given the choice.

But my intention was not to put any expectations on the situation or, most importantly, my performance. Because of that one stipulation, I relaxed more—a lot more, in fact. Just showing up was enough to begin with.

The outings didn't always go great. But, whereas in the past, I would cringe at the thought and vow never to be seen in public again, I learned from each encounter and was fine with it, I had never experienced anything like this before and I felt normal again. This thermostat shift has to come from within to stick. So be kind to yourself while taking small steps forward without judgment. Eventually, without notice, your thermostat will be set at awesome!

One of the events I attended during this time gave me an incredible insight. As I was journaling my three pages that day (which was another challenge from the book), I started with a negative rundown of how I had completely messed up my night, starting with the fact that I drank wine. Not excessively, but even one drink (okay, two) tends to make me a hundred and fifty pounds fatter and disrupts my sleep and attitude the next day. Not a good idea for an introvert who needs energy and to be able to get in and out of seats.

As I was writing this down in my journal, I suddenly realized what was happening. I was doing my usual cringing and berating myself for things that I had or hadn't said or having done or not done the right thing. Not that any of what I did was bad or that I had offended anyone, but I was playing in my mind possible scenarios in which someone could have taken what I said the wrong way, etc. Or things I could've said that would have been much better (ever done that?). Suddenly my mind went crazy and out of control onto all sorts of memories of the cringe-worthy times in my life. It was like I was going through my entire library of mishaps. This was even worse than I normally would do.

Then the insight hit me.

When I was coaching people on health and fitness, I would sometimes get my clients (and myself periodically) to do a detox; an elimination diet that would cut out toxins and allow the body to flush out the remaining stored toxins from the fat cells. These toxins would only be able to be released when there was no additional toxins coming into the body. What I would make clear to my clients was that, initially, they would *not* feel better. In fact, they will probably feel like shit because all those stored toxins were going to be running through the bloodstream to be flushed out. If they were aware, they wouldn't freak out and they would be able to continue knowing that even though they were not feeling great, it was for a great reason.

It struck me that I was going through a mental detox. My mind was flushing out memory after memory of "toxic" thoughts.

I had been constantly noticing my thinking and reminding myself that it was judgment. Not doing anything about it, simply noticing.

This habit was taking effect, because the whole time I was thinking these thoughts of the past, I kept saying in my mind *it's just a judgment* and would let them go.

In the morning, I realized what was going on and how I had handled it. (This was about 3:00 in the morning, by the way.) Yet I didn't go into my pity pot or think I was worthless and a failure. I didn't feel good, I admit, but it wasn't as debilitating as it would have been in the past.

I wasn't feeling great, but it was for a great reason.

This made so much sense as my clients (and myself) have often experienced that when things started to go well and they felt like they were "getting it," suddenly World War III was declared, and an avalanche of toxic thoughts and habits started flowing back.

Previously, I just thought that this process was the ego thermostat fighting to get back to homeostasis. But now I see that it is our mind cleansing out the shit thoughts, and if we just stick with it, noticing without judgment, we will get to the good stuff of the cleanse: clarity, energy, and "weight loss" in terms of losing those thoughts that weigh us down, of course—although you never know. Seriously, it's not uncommon to shed excess weight as well as excess baggage in the mind because your mind and body are working efficiently, letting go of the inflammation caused by this toxicity. The new thermostat set point is now being allowed to be set in place.

The reason I'm writing this is not to say, "look at me." Okay, maybe a little, but mainly to highlight what happened to not just me, but a lot of my clients, and what can happen for you and your life when you get out of your own way. This is possibly not far from what you are already doing. The life-changing difference here is noticing without the judgment.

There's a great Chinese fable about a farmer and his son who owned only one workhorse, which they heavily relied on for farming. One day, the horse escaped and was nowhere to be found. When the neighbors heard of this, they gathered around and commiserated with the farmer over his bad luck, to which the farmer said, "Good luck, bad luck, who knows?"

A few days later, the horse returned with a herd of wild horses following. The neighbors congratulate him on such good luck, but he said (say it with me), "Good luck, bad luck, who knows?"

The farmer's son was taming one of the wild horses when he was thrown off and broke his leg. The neighbors all agreed *what bad luck this was.* But the farmer said (sing it), "Good luck, bad luck, who knows?"

A couple of weeks later, the army marched into the village, looking for all young men to fight in a civil war that was happening, forcing them to enlist. They saw the farmer's son with the broken leg and realized that he would be no use in battle, so they left him alone. The neighbors, of course, were amazed at the good fortune of the farmer, but he said (altogether now), "Good luck, bad luck, who knows?"

Let go of judgment.

Huh?

- Respect your thermostat. Most people are more like thermometers, letting circumstances dictate how they feel. You cannot override it with just self-help tactics and strategies. It's like trying to dry yourself while still in the shower and it's turned on. You turn the shower off by turning the judgments off.

- Your thermostat sets the "temperature" of your life. It takes a little practice of getting out of the way to get it to where you want it to be, but it doesn't need your help once you've set it, you get rid of the shit so that your diamond sets your thermostat. When you notice without judgment, miraculous things start to happen.

- If you judge and try to say, "stop it," you are judging the judging.

- You may experience even more thoughts at first when letting go of judgments, because you may be beginning a mental (shit) detox. Just focus on how good you will feel once all that ego shit is gone.

You won't necessarily feel great, but it's for a great reason.

Thermostat Training

Set a timer for one minute, three times each day. In this minute, take a few deep breaths in and out through the nose. Imagine breathing into your heart, then simply notice your thinking, feelings, or anything going on within you. You may notice yourself dwelling on the fact that the damn air conditioner isn't working properly (okay that's my stuff) or whatever comes up. Practice noticing without trying to fix or judge in any way, not even labeling anything that comes up as good or bad (who knows). This may be tough at first, so don't beat yourself up over it, just do the best that you can. If a minute is too much, start with twenty seconds and gradually build up. Remember to do things in baby steps to set yourself up to win.

On the surface this may not seem like it's doing much, but consistency is key. This will break the mirage and bring you back to your diamond thermostatic setting. Remember that the diamond does not experience anxiety, that's just the shit.

I challenge you to also go on a mental detox occasionally. Start with twenty-four hours without TV, reading, or even music. If twenty-four hours is too much, try two hours. The more often you do this the easier and more effective it will be. This to me is as effective as meditating. It can even enhance your meditation if you are meditating already.

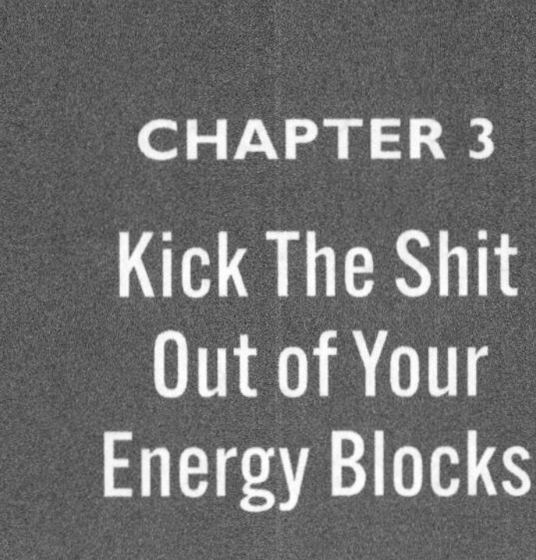

"If everything is energy, including ourselves,
then we are all connected to everything."

LEE VALLELY

If you are wondering why the heck I am talking about esoteric thinking when this is supposed to be a book about "breaking free of the socially distanced self," I wouldn't blame you. But there *is* a reason, and it's what makes this book different. Rather than just changing your thinking for a short time, it changes your paradigm—your thermostat. This is about *being*, not *doing*. Not just a temporary feel-good in the moment but doesn't really create a lasting lifestyle. A permanent change.

There are two main ways of thinking in the world. The horizontal way of thinking tends to deal with what is in front of us—the "seeing is believing" practical, materialistic, everyday experiences. Then there is the vertical way of thinking that looks beyond the physical, beyond even the identity, and goes to a spiritual answer to the question, "Who am I?"

If we get stuck thinking in just one of these ways, it can create a problem. Alternatively, when we think in both ways, we create a very flexible way of thinking, hence making problem solving ridiculously easier (I didn't say easy so don't shoot me). Problem solving is only necessary when there's a problem. With flexible thinking, you are much more resilient, and a lot of "problems" dissolve because they become well within your comfort zone. When your comfort zone increases, situations that were classed as problems are well within your capabilities and so not really what you would classify as a problem.

Kick the Shit Out of Interference

In a past life (mentally, not physically), I coached kids who played tennis at a high level. I really loved this book called *The Inner Game of Tennis* by Timothy Gallway.[15] I used the teachings of the book for a lot of my coaching. What's weird is, I must have read that book at least three or four times, yet it wasn't until Jamie Smart, a phenomenal speaker and author of many amazing books including *Clarity*,[16] wrote out the following equation from *The Inner Game of Tennis* book, that I realized the importance of it, and is now an equation I remind myself of daily:

Potential - Interference = Performance

Potential is infinite. On a physical level, you might say that there are limitations, yet it has been said (though not everyone agrees) that we only use 10 percent or so of our brain's capacity, which leaves a lot of potential left for us to discover. Potential is our true self, our diamond. What makes it seem impossible are our limiting beliefs (shit) around the subject. The shit is the interference.

The interference is the judgments, labels, comparisons, ideals, assumptions, and beliefs about what we can and cannot do, be, or have. In other words, it's the illusionary shit that surrounds our diamond. It can also be the paint that poorly impersonates the diamond, leading us to believe that our accomplishments, title, etc. are our true self, rather than the diamond. So, we work harder and harder to look better and accomplish more, painting over our shit, thinking that this is the only way that we can be worthy, not realizing that not only is this not necessary, but this is also a very poor imitation of the truth and taking us further away from it. We are already worthy and can shine so brightly that we need no artificial paint whatsoever. With this understanding, we accomplish and grow because we are inspired to do so, without fearing any judgment if we don't.

So, my equation is this:

Potential (Diamond) – Interference (shit) = Performance (the creation you bring to the world)

Sydney Banks, an enlightened man and author of six books including *The Enlightened Gardener*,[17] said that when you take away judgment, what's left is pure love. The word love can be incredibly misunderstood. Often when we talk about love, it's with an agenda. Probably the closest we see to unconditional love is between a mother and child, and even then, it's not always unconditional.

Another word you could easily use is energy, or you might use joy, or peace, or appreciation. The list could go on because, at their core, they are all similar feelings (resonance, frequency, vibration). It's where we touch our innate well-being, the diamond. This, contrary to popular belief, is our natural state. But . . . it's not our "normal" state, unfortunately.

If I asked a hundred people what they would default to if they left their thoughts and feelings to their own devices, most, including myself not so long ago, would say that they would go to some form of negative thoughts—worry, anxiety, sadness, and maybe even depression. It looks like that's our underlying natural state, but it's actually a constantly learned behavior; it is *not* natural!

Kick the Shit Out of Pressure

Why do angels fly? Because they take themselves lightly.

Okay, what the heck do you do with that? I'll tell you what: you take the pressure off yourself, that's what. The pressure you place on yourself is what is holding you back, that's the shit interference. Not the circumstances. Not the debilitating anxiety. Not the fear of not being enough or not belonging. Not the crappy childhood you had. Not the body you were given. You may feel like you were shortchanged in some way, but that's not what's preventing you from having a wonderful life. You cannot go back and change the past, but you can make the rest of your life fun lovingly spectacular.

This is not to say you should be a Pollyanna, pretending everything is wonderful when you don't really believe it, but when you are in a low vibration/energy (meaning a low state of consciousness or a low mood), you can only see problems, and solutions are not even visible to you. When you are in a higher vibration/consciousness/mood/energy, you can only see solutions and will not get stuck in the problems.

Please stick with this! It's so much more powerful than only having the horizontal, materialistic way of thinking, which tends to be separated from the spiritual aspect of the psyche and focused more on the mechanics, thinking you're the victim of your life instead of its creator. Being totally vertical in your thinking (nothing exists and it's all an illusion for instance), can also be detrimental at times. It's very hard to balance a check book in this way of thinking. Getting the balance right is the key to a happy, healthy, anxiety-free life. But let's face it, we've got the horizontal thinking down, don't you think? So, we want to get the vertical thinking down predominantly. As we discuss this vertical thinking, the balancing of the two takes care of itself.

Our consciousness is energy, vibration, frequency, and resonance. When we raise our consciousness, we raise our energy. This raises our thermostat automatically.

Everything in this universe is made of energy, as a wise person stated, and he knew his stuff. Light has a super-fast vibration for instance, whereas something like a rock has a much lower vibration. We all have varying frequency/vibration. Our thoughts, emotions, and feelings are constantly dictating our vibration. (Vibration refers to the oscillating and vibrating movement of atoms and particles caused by energy. Frequency is the rate at which the vibrations and oscillations occur. So, I will refer to either, meaning the same thing).

Frequency attracts similar frequencies. Think of it like tuning an old radio or TV. There's a certain frequency that connects to that station. If you want to listen to 101 FM, but you are tuned to 98.2, you are not going to hear that cool song that's playing, no matter how hard you listen. As soon as you switch your dial to 101 FM, your radio receives the signal vibrating at that frequency.

This is obvious now that we've had radios for over a hundred years. But what if you didn't know about frequency? The horizontal way of thinking may get you to believe that it's the radio's fault and it needs to be fixed, not realizing that you just need to adjust the dial.

We sometimes think that we, too, are faulty and need to be fixed. But when you understand that it's simply a frequency issue, then you understand that it's just a simple adjustment of the dial needed to change your frequency. No major repairs are necessary.

We can make a positive shift in our lives and our connections by shifting our frequency. We not only have a frequency, but, just like the radio station, we emit a frequency out into the world.

Ever known someone who you would consider vibrant? They're vibrating at a high frequency. Ever encountered an "energy vampire?" Guess what, they're vibrating at a low

frequency. You can learn all the techniques in the world, say all the right things, look the part, but if you have a crappy frequency, people will feel it. I'm living proof. I had the "Tony Robbins" script memorized, but no one (okay maybe my mom) would listen. The killer is that other people may also be emitting that low frequency, so you connect only to people at a low-level frequency. Now, all you have is two or more people emitting crappy frequencies. Not very fulfilling. Ever known a person who seems to "attract" the same kind of relationships? Or the people who love to bitch and moan about the world together?

As we take things lightly, and naturally shift our vibration through the fundamental understanding that we are not broken, just dealing with some shit, we can lift the shit veil that is covering our diamond, and our natural frequency becomes our new thermostat setting.

Kick The Shit Out of Your Life and Watch Your Frequency Rise

Where are you on an energy frequency scale? For me it's stable though still fluctuates a little, whereas previously it used to fluctuate crazily. I remember that I used to try to tell jokes, but I would tell the punchline in the wrong place and apologize profusely, getting embarrassed (rather than what I do now because I'm still saying the punchline in the wrong place but now I just make fun of my joke-telling). Or worse someone would tell a great story and get everyone in a good mood, then I would say something that just turned the humor into a serious, low-energy feeling. I was that energy vampire.

I was trying to portray a high frequency while feeling in a low frequency, which can't be done. My thermostat was wonky, and my shit was starting to show. So, I tried to cover it up with some joke-telling "paint." I thought my radio needed fixing and I felt at the mercy of my crappy frequency, thinking it was out of my control.

But you are the creator of your vibration, you can turn the dial on your metaphorical radio. You are not at the mercy of listening to a crappy talk radio show for the rest of your life.

You can be the change that you wish to see, simply by a conscious understanding and tweaking of your feelings, which is the barometer of your vibration/frequency.

There are levels of energy where people can naturally transform the frequency of others around them through their own higher vibrational frequency.

Did you get that? I don't think you did.

They change the energy of the people who encounter them. Not because of what they say or do, or how good their jokes are, but because they are emanating a beautiful higher frequency than that of most people around them, so it enhances (albeit temporary) the frequencies of the people who encounter them. That's so much more powerful than being a great joke teller (although both is even better). People often talk about being uplifted just by being in the presence of Indian gurus, etc. Unfortunately, a lot of people then go back to the way they were, thinking that it's only in the presence of the guru that they can feel this way.

The average frequency rating of the entire world now is 204hz.

According to research by Dr. David Hawkins, author of the most informative books on this topic, like *Power vs. Force*,[18] 78 percent of the world's population register below 200hz on this scale of consciousness (don't get overwhelmed by the numbers, it will make sense by the end of this), below the frequency at which truth and integrity are present.

It is scary to think that most people on the planet are working with a lower frequency than honesty and integrity. By this statistic, only 22 percent of the population of the world is even capable of experientially acting from truth. Anything below 200 tends to create a negative energy, meaning that most people are consuming rather than emitting energy. Little wonder we introverts (loosely meaning we tend to recharge most of our energy being alone rather than from others) can get so exhausted when around lots of people. You cannot replenish lost energy, plus you may be at a deficit yourself. So, it's a lose-lose situation, where the introvert is at a deficit by being around people, and then if the people are below a 200 vibration, they will be extracting even more energy.

So, when we talk about a massive change, it is beyond imagination what can take place in your life merely by letting go of some old shit and allowing your vibration to rise naturally.

As little as 2 percent of the population of the world reaches the level of the frequency of love, which is 500. This is not unconditional love, which is 540 and which is equal to joy, and is only enjoyed by 0.4 percent of the population.

Do you see the scale of this? Just by raising your vibration/consciousness/ frequency, even just a few points upward beyond the 200, or just a few points above wherever you are now, you become a more unique individual. Someone who, merely by your being, makes a difference in the world so the quality of your life, and the lives of those around you, will improve.

When you raise your consciousness, you counteract the negative overall energy of people around you. According to the scale by Dr. David Hawkins, at a level of just 300, you counteract the possible negative energy of 90,000 people in your presence. At 500, the level of love, you counteract the possible negative energy of 750,000 people who are below 200. That's some serious, life-changing stuff! I highly recommend the book *Power vs. Force* by Dr. David R. Hawkins, as well as *The Eye of the I*, where you can get an understanding of the enormity of this realization.

What's great about this is that you don't have to do anything. It's more about not doing, not getting in the way of your true self, letting go—realizing that when you let go of the illusionary shit surrounding you, your energy naturally rises like a helium filled balloon.

When you drop the illusionary barriers, you will naturally have an increase in your frequency/vibration because you return to your natural state. This takes practice, not because it's hard, but because we're creatures of habit and we tend to fall back into stinking thinking. (As I'm writing this, I suddenly noticed the time and thought immediately that I must rest because we are meeting someone in a couple of hours, believing that I must conserve my energy. It's so funny how we make up shit without being aware of it, but once we know the truth, it has no power. Now I simply notice and am amused by it. Okay now I'll take a nap.)

When we learn that our personality is made up and becomes so painful to accept, we can hit a fork in the road. One way, the vertical way, dissolves the hold of ego or personality (which btw are the same thing) and rises in vibration. The other, more common way is to split the personality to create an alter ego. This way the ego is preserved but the personality is shared between one type, then another type of personality. People can be "two-faced" or a "Jekyll and Hyde." Some evangelists and fundamentalists can mistakenly fall into this trap. The label bipolar can be a symptom of this.

This is partly (almost entirely) why some people have multiple personalities (although, that describes almost everyone on the planet). They can create such a personality that it is almost impossible to distinguish from their "real" one if you don't know their history. Why? Because there is no real personality. We make this shit up, yet we will fight to the death to protect it.

I remember coming to the end of the series *King of Queens*[19] with the hilarious Kevin James and the beautiful and hilarious Leah Remini. Oh, and let's not forget the amazing character by Jerry Stiller! When I watched the last episode, I felt sad. It was like I had lost my friends. But they were actors! They don't know that I exist, and their characters don't exist anyway. Yet I mourned the "death," in a sense, of the characters they played. (By the way, this series ended almost twenty years ago, yet I only watched the last episode recently.) This is no different than mourning the "death" of your earlier personality, it's just as made up as the characters in *King of Queens.*

Do you believe that you have the identical personality as you had when you were five? Yes, you have memories, perhaps, that were attributed to who you were when you were five. But even then, can you rely on those memories being 100 percent true? The personality has drastically changed. The shit has accumulated, the paint has thickened, the beliefs have set, preferences have increased, changing your personality. But you are still you, not your personality. The diamond is the same, ageless, intact, regardless of circumstances or time.

When you start to get out of your own way, you will naturally let go of your ego. It will still be there, but like a laptop is there when necessary to use, not something to dictate everything that you think, attract, do, or say in your life. Your consciousness will rise, and consequently, you will notice that people are more drawn to you. It's called the Law of Attraction for a reason, like magnetism. Poverty comes from an inner poverty frequency; wealth comes from inner wealth frequency. Love from an inner love frequency.

Dogs know, people know. We've all heard of the person who doesn't play by the rules, who doesn't care. "The rebel without a cause." They tend to be attractive to a lot of people. But we don't have to be rebels without a cause to let go of resistance and can still be caring, loving, and generous people without all the shit.

I went to a seminar once where a person on the stage was blindfolded. Then the audience were tasked with the best way to show the person how to get to the back of the room.

After many ingenious ways to assist this person to be guided to the back of the room unscathed, one of the audience simply asked the person to take the blindfold off.

Life is so much easier to navigate when we take off the shit blindfold.

Kick The Shit Out of Life and "Live Like Sean"

A few years ago, I joined a local gym. A young guy, I would say in his mid-twenties, came up to me. He had special needs, which was not obvious at first, but as he spoke there was a distortion in his face and speech. What hit me though was the beautiful conversation that I had with him. I have no idea what we spoke about, I do remember that he said that he hadn't seen me in the gym before, so clearly wanted to know everything about me and tell me everything about him. Once he gave me his information, he said that we would talk again, then moved on to the next person that needed his attention. I loved our interaction, and it brought a smile to my day. I never really thought anything more than what a beautiful encounter that was. Until we met our friend TJ Nelligan.

He wrote a book, that I highly, highly, in fact, insist that you read called *Live Like Sean*.[20]

Not because he is my buddy, but because this is a book that will show you absolutely everything that you ever need to know about connecting and being sociable with others. How to love and be loved.

The book is about his amazing son and the way he made people feel in his presence.

This book taught me so many lessons, and the one that really stands out for me is that he really loved people (not absolutely everyone however, and that was a valuable lesson also, how he had an instinct to stay away from certain people, but this was very few and very far between).

I won't tell the stories here because I couldn't do them justice and it is going to tap into your heart when you read the book. What struck me was how easily we can take people, and ourselves, for granted because we are stuck in our heads most of the time, judging people, places, and things, including, and sometimes especially, ourselves.

I had heard this expression many times, but when I read this book, I realized the importance of it. People, that includes you and me, want to be loved and appreciated.

Big wow, you've heard that a thousand times perhaps. But when we are in our heads, worrying about the future or dwelling on the past, we are not only not appreciating or loving ourselves, but we are missing vital opportunities to give this love  and appreciation to the hundreds (possibly) of people that we interact with, sometimes without ever even knowing their names. It doesn't take a lot to show appreciation to someone. Just being present is more than enough. By being present, rather than in your thoughts, you are showing that person that they exist in your world. By smiling, you are appreciating them, and, in a subtle way, you are showing them love. Some people, especially women (which I can appreciate), are afraid of giving the wrong impression. But don't let a few misinterpretations cause you to dim your light on others or yourself. Live like Sean. He was a beacon of light and love, and by his example, you can be too.

Say Again?

- There's a horizontal, stuck-in-the-matrix, seeing-is-believing way of thinking. Then there's the vertical, beyond-identity way of thinking. Both are necessary to create a balance, though we tend to have mastered the horizontal. The more we can see above the maze through vertical thinking, the more our comfort zone, therefore our thermostat, increases.

- You don't need the horizontal thinking of tactics and strategies to make a difference in your world or the people around you, just take the shit blindfold off and see from the vertical height of loving and feeling loved.

- Burn this into your mind: **Potential(diamond) – interference(shit) = Performance**. When we clear the interference (shit), we allow our full potential to be our go-to.

- Our vibrational frequencies are energy. The less interference, the higher that energy goes. That's when we become the change that we wish to see in the world.

- Live like Sean. People love people who love people. So just love people. After all, that's all anybody, including yourself, ever needs.

A Shit Exercise

Potential – Interference = Performance

Potential is taken care of, so let's determine what the interference is.

Take a deep breath in, hold it for a few seconds, then as you breathe out just say to yourself, in your mind, "Let go." Think of something you would love to achieve, do, or be. It can be anything, like being comfortable at a social event, speaking on stage, or maybe being the life and soul of the party. Notice your feelings and thoughts, and maybe say something to yourself. Notice as if you are observing yourself doing this. You don't have to remember the words, feelings, or anything, just notice yourself noticing these thoughts, feelings, or voices. This is all the shit that's holding you back. Now take in that deep breath again, hold it as you notice all that shit, then in your mind, say to yourself "let go." Now, just like when you really go full force in the toilet, let go. It may take a few flushes to let this shit go. No need to be perfect. You may struggle at first, that's okay, just let that go too. The key here is not to label or judge anything, especially yourself.

Do this anytime. At first you may want to close your eyes and get a feel for it, but after a while, as soon as you notice some interference, be that a problem, a feeling, or you find yourself saying something negative to yourself or others even, you can simply take a deep breath in, hold momentarily as you see the interference, and say "let go" in your mind as you breathe out.

Please practice this now and forever; practice makes perfect. Then, when you need it most, you will be a master of letting go.

CHAPTER 4

Kick The Shit Out of Your Map: Tap into Your Inner GPS

"Your intellect is not you; it is merely
a tool. So, if you identify yourself
as an intellectual, *you* are a tool 😁"

LEE VALLELY

Take a deep breath in through your nose, hold that breath just a little while. Now let that breath go. Breathe in again and imagine breathing into your heart area. Hold for just as long as is comfortable for you, keeping your attention on your heart area, and let that breath go. Notice how this helps you get into a more relaxed and less heady state of mind. Keep going if it feels comfortable.

Have you ever had a gut feeling or instinct to do or not do something? Did you ever regret not listening to that inner voice? Or, on the flip side, have you ever regretted listening to that inner voice?

While most of us would answer yes to the first and second questions, I've rarely heard of someone saying they *regretted* listening to their inner voice. In very rare cases when someone says that they did, indeed, regret it or it turned out badly, when we dig further, it was usually not wisdom, alias inner GPS, but fear talking.

And when I say fear, I'm not referring to pure fear, because that is actually tapped into wisdom. I'm talking about worry, anxiety, stress, and ego.

Remember that I'm referring to the beginning stages of practicing listening to your inner voice. As people get more and more aware and intuitive, they can see, hear, and feel their inner GPS with great clarity. Even smell and taste can play a role as the wisdom gets clearer.

Your GPS has two coordinates: where you are and where you want to go. Both are without judgment. Just like my British lady GPS in my car, who's very patient with me, though I sense a hint of sarcasm in her voice.

When we simply look at the facts, just the facts, and then go in the direction of whatever our GPS tells us, the GPS will be constantly monitoring where we are and adjust accordingly. That's something that a map, goal, plan, strategy, or personal intellect cannot do.

You Are Here

I went to Disneyland years ago with my wife Andi and my stepdaughter Talia. As you know, there are many boards around the area saying "you are here" showing where you are in the park so you can figure out which direction to head in. We were away from the signs just sitting on a wall. Talia was looking at the customary paper map they gave us at the beginning, trying to figure out where we were and how to get to the next ride. Andi impatiently told her to look for the "you are here" sign on the paper map. Her daughter looked at her in disbelief and said, "Mom! It's a map!"

Although that was a very funny moment (okay, maybe you had to be there), we all metaphorically fall into that trap of presuming that the "you are here" sign is on our made-up paper map.

We mistake our presumptions of the "virtual map," alias looking through our assumptions and beliefs (shit) for the "you are here" sign. We even fear looking at where we are sometimes because it's too scary, with all judgments and presumptions, thinking that the truth is too horrible to accept. We can so often exaggerate how bad things are now, and underestimate how fantastic we can make things be in the future. This leads us to live from a faulty map with an illusionary "you are here" sign.

I hear so many clients express how they cannot find any friends because people just want to take advantage of them and they can't trust people. This is a made-up "you are here" sign. Using this as their starter point, is it any wonder that they struggle to find "real" friends?

We can sometimes believe that we must analyze every detail in order to make a decision, which can sometimes cause paralysis by analysis. Especially as the "you are here" sign, based on our past judgments, is starting from the completely wrong place, made up from shit filters.

Imagine if you had the choice between two laptops. The first one has 3 TB of space and all the bells and whistles built into the system—it's a beast of a machine. However, it has one vital flaw: it has no capability for internet access whatsoever, which is unheard of now. The other is a basic laptop with a decent speed but very limited memory. The two things it has going for it though is that it has constant, twenty-four seven access to the internet and is solar powered. So, you can be on a desert island, or even a cruise, and get full access to the internet.

Which one would you choose?

Almost all of us would choose the latter because it's much better to have the latest, most up-to-date information at your fingertips.

The information that is up to date now, no matter how cutting edge, will eventually be out of date, like most of our beliefs, for instance. (Still believe in the tooth fairy? Yeah, me too.)

Now some intellectuals may have valid arguments as to why the more powerful laptop may have its advantages; however, it's going to be difficult to override the fact that it is not connected to universal intelligence.

Five-time *New York Times* bestselling author and scientist Greg Braden, who's latest book *The Wisdom Codes*[21] is positively life-changing, says that the heart is 5,000 times more perceptive than the brain, and this guy knows his stuff.

Here's the bittersweet news: we have that top-of-the-line laptop called our mind. But this top-of-the-line laptop also has access to the internet of life, or universal intelligence. That's the fantastic news. Unfortunately, most of us have been trained to switch off the internet and rely on the information stored on our laptops, alias our shit beliefs (especially if we consider ourselves to be intellectuals). Worse still, we can believe this information to be fact or the up-to-date information—like the "you are here" sign.

I recently found out that a belief I had had since I was about ten years old was completely, and very obviously, wrong—to the point that it's ridiculously embarrassing, so don't tell anyone. I was told as a kid that, in England, the public schools were the top schools that most people paid for and wanted to go to, whereas the private schools were the not-so-good schools that no one wanted to go to.

I still can't believe that I thought that; it doesn't even make sense. But I was a naive kid so I believed those well-meaning adults, to such an extent that even my common sense couldn't override it. I promise you that, as ridiculous as it sounds, I didn't discover this belief was wrong until a few years ago. Don't judge me.

When we come into this world, we are helpless. We rely totally on others to wipe our bottoms and feed and clothe us (some of us still do, in a way). At first, people rally around to keep us amused and happy. If they cry, most babies get immediate attention. We make a face and get applause from people. We can do no wrong . . . until that fateful day when we're old enough to be responsible for our actions, and the stuff that we once got applause for is not so cute anymore. This is a shock to the system. We hear the word "no" for the first time.

What the heck does that word mean?

We will hear that word many, many thousands more times. So, we adjust our actions accordingly. Our beliefs are molded by what we are told by our peers, guardians, teachers, and parents, as well as our experiences, good or bad. This is what I call our intellectual life. Prior to this, we were unaware of the intellectual, rational thinking, judging, and labeling mind—the horizontal way of thinking. We were still in the analog, hypnotic, creative, curious mindset—the vertical way of thinking.

If you were to ask a class of five-year-old kids how many were creative or artistic, almost every hand would go up. Ask that same group at eleven years old and maybe half, if that, might raise their hands. Ask them at sixteen years old and less than a handful might admit to it. Did they come to their senses or was there some learned behavior (accumulated shit) involved? No wonder we go into a social event with a shitload of outdated information, expecting a (usually not so great) result before we even enter the situation.[22]

Babies and animals seem to live predominantly by instinct, and of course, we feel superior to them for obvious reasons. We have a prefrontal cortex, which gives us the opportunity to think, rationalize, etc. We can speak, which gives us far superior communication skills. The concept of going back to listening to wisdom is sometimes misinterpreted as going back to just living by instinct alone. But societally, most of us have been taught to literally bypass our innate wisdom and rely almost entirely on our intellect, choosing the laptop without the universal internet. Most people think that talking about this is too woo-woo; they are afraid of being thought of as a weirdo. But don't you think it's even weirder that we would be taught to switch off our most powerful advisor? If you were to do this without realizing you were missing out on all this wisdom, wouldn't you want someone to tell you? To wake you up to it? Well, hello, it's Lee, here's your wakeup call!

Is it Intuition or Ego?

So where do you think your inner GPS is coming from? And how TF do you know whether it is your inner GPS guiding you, or if it's the intellect or ego (which is one and the same) in disguise?

The first, easiest, and almost foolproof way to determine this is to check if there's a story attached to the feedback. The ego *loves* stories, but the GPS is straight to the point. It's a yes or no, or even just a knowing. It's neither positive nor negative. It just says yes, no, turn left at the next exit.

Here's another tip to differentiate ego from intuition: remember that your intuition doesn't (I'm going to sound very American here) think you suck. Never does your intuitive mind think you suck, because at your core you are whole. You are the diamond. There is nothing about you that sucks, so if that's what you're hearing, then I can 100 percent guarantee that it's not your intuition communicating.

Our egos are so obsessed with our false identity that we want to dig deeper and find the faults and the causes of why we're broken so that we can be better people, parents, children, lawyers, sex goddesses, whatever it is. Myself very much included. This is the ego believing it's not perfect.

Don't get me wrong; I'm not talking about learning skills. You can improve your skills in various roles. You need to learn to walk and ride a bike, but that's different from needing to fix you. You don't need fixing; you don't need to improve your self-esteem.

That's a tough one for people to grasp. You might think that I really don't know you, so how can I make that assumption? What I do know is that you are perfectly you, you perfect diamond you.

I "suffered" from insecurities and shyness—social anxiety—my whole life. Confidence was something others had and I, as much as I could, just pretended that I had it. But as soon as anyone questioned that confidence, I broke down, scuttling to the closest dark place like a cockroach. I am not saying that if you saw me now, you would think that I was just oozing confidence, but I hope that you would notice that I am comfortable in my own skin. This is something I had not experienced before in my life that I can remember—oh, except when I did that amazing performance from the sofa, of course. I've still got the underwear that was thrown at me.

Just kidding . . . I haven't got the underwear . . . anymore.

I know that I am not my behavior. I am not my judgments or anybody else's judgments. If my behavior is not good, I can correct it. But it has no bearing on who I am at my core, or on my worthiness. So, the idea of working on my self-worth, which I had been doing unsuccessfully for most of my life, seems ludicrous to me now.

The truth shall set you free, and the inner GPS will always give you truth and correct guidance, from the truth that you are perfect as you are. That . . . is the "you are here" sign.

A few years ago, I had what, to me and my wife, was an obvious example of my inner GPS in action. I was invited to attend this talk by a self-help type of person I had not heard of previously. It's no surprise that I was interested because I often listen to people who have been recommended to me. But if you, like me, have suffered from social fear, you will understand the uniqueness of the situation that unfolded.

We could attend the talk either in person or via Zoom. If we went in person, we would be paying over double because there were two of us, plus it was a forty-minute drive each way, so the obvious solution would be Zoom. That would have been music to my ears normally, but (I still can't believe that I did this) I convinced my wife that we needed to go in person, even though she was tired and didn't feel like "schlepping." I don't know why I insisted on going in person; this was at the end of a long day. Andi is normally the one who tries to talk me into going to these things, yet on this occasion, she was not in the mood to go. If you know what it's like to feel uncomfortable, you know that her not wanting to go, giving me the excuse to get out of having to put myself through possible hell, would have felt like me being freed from captivity and winning the lottery at the same time.

But I insisted that we go!? I am still amazed by this. Nothing about our going made any sense, not even a desire to hear what this speaker had to say, but I just knew that we needed to go in person. So, I metaphorically dragged my wife out by her hair, kicking and screaming, and off we went.

When we got there, the place was packed; it was being hosted in a private home. This was not a good start for me. Everyone was already seated since we arrived slightly late, so all eyes were on us as we walked in. The presenter (on Zoom) even stopped for a moment. I was dying inside.

We then realized that we had just driven for forty minutes, and paid double the price for the privilege, to find out that the speaker was on a Zoom call!

So, we were sitting in a stranger's house, after disturbing everyone, watching a Zoom screen that we could've been watching in the comfort and safety of our own home!

At this point, I doubted my GPS. I figured I must've had a faulty connection or something. The talk was nice. (I can't say I got anything necessarily life-changing from the talk. Don't get me wrong, it was good, just not *that* good.) But by the time the talk had ended and we drove home at the end of the night, we knew why we went there.

The home we were in was Lisa and David's home, two of our now dearest friends to this day.

Lisa McCourt is part of my inspiration for this book. She is the author of, among many other books, *Juicy Joy,* and her latest phenomenal book *Free Your Joy.*[23] She is a very well-established Hay House writer and editor and has sold millions of copies in her time. Lisa gave me lots of great ideas about how to edit, publish, etc., the ins and outs of writing. Andi and I have spoken at her events. We have been introduced to so many wonderful people because of meeting and befriending these two incredible souls, and we cherish the fact that by some miracle, I listened to my inner GPS that night, even though it made no sense whatsoever at the time. Countless serendipitous moments have happened because of going to their house that evening. We both know that it was 100 percent my inner GPS guiding me to go there that evening.

There have been many, many instances where we have listened to our GPS and it has had miraculous consequences for us. Maybe I'll share these with you one day. The reason I chose this one is because of how obvious it was, knowing how much of a miracle this was for me to do, having always suffered from social fear. I bet you have a story like this, too. I would love to hear it.

Seriously, if you do have a story, please contact me: www.shifthappens.global or contact me on social media.

We may glance at wisdom, but most of us don't even notice.

I'm sure you've heard the expression that if you give a person a fish, they may eat for one day, but teach a person to fish and they can feed themselves for a lifetime. By learning a strategy, you may be okay in a situation or two. But by understanding that you have this built-in GPS that will always point you in the right direction, you now know how to fish for a lifetime of being so much more than just okay.

Do What Now?

- You have two laptops at your fingertips, your super-duper intellect, and your GPS internet. The good news is you don't have to choose; you can use both. This is the balance of horizontal and vertical thinking.

- Notice what you are paying attention to. Is it your shit or your GPS? If there's a story attached to the information, it's not wisdom speaking, it's your ego.

- Your inner GPS (wisdom) doesn't think you suck. Knowing this allows you to be in any situation, knowing that you will be very much okay, having natural self-esteem and an assurance that, after some practice, perhaps you will know when you are heading in the right direction.

Let's practice:

- Think of a time when you listened to your GPS. Remember how you knew it was intuition as opposed to intellect or ego? Think of situations where you may have done something different, or perhaps not done something which you normally would have. Just noticing how you have intuition will allow you to tap into it more frequently and rely on it more often.

- I have never met a person who hasn't had some sort of intuitive experience, big or small, be it a flash of thoughts or insight, a voice, or a feeling. Yet most people, it seems, are hesitant, if not afraid, to go by intuition due to societal conditioning. Hence a lot of anxiety, often caused by confusion of some description. So, break this pattern. Start to pay attention to the little nudges here and there. Don't drive yourself crazy with it, just setting the intention will allow you to be more observant.

As we did at the start of this chapter, let's take a deep breath in through the nose. Hold it for a second or two, then let go and breathe out. Now take three deep breaths like this. This time imagine breathing into your heart. Your heart is the predominant area of your intuition. On the third breath, think of a question that you would like to be intuitively answered. It can be as trivial as what you should eat for dinner, or as important as what you ought to do with the rest of your life. It's your choice. However, my advice would be to practice a little before hitting the big questions.

Do this often to get used to the feeling and improve your connection. Let me know how it goes.

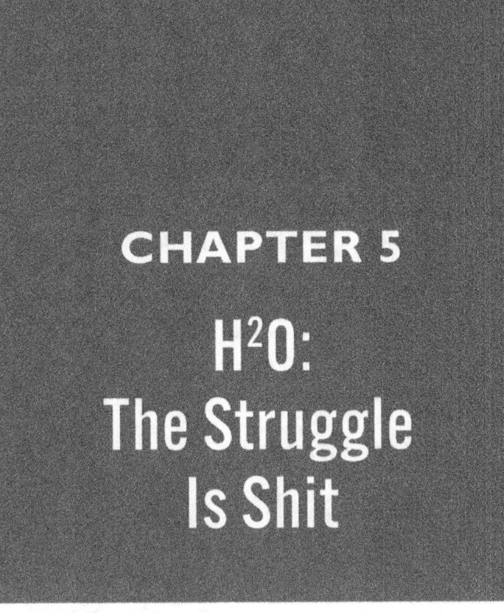

> *"It is not the strongest of the species
> that survives, nor the most intelligent,
> but the one most responsive to change."*[24]

CHARLES DARWIN

This is going to simplify and change your life, for the better. We are going deep, and just like in the film *The Matrix*,[25] you are about to take the red pill. Or is it the blue pill? Whichever pill frees your mind.

Do you realize that we each live in a separate world, created in our mind? This world is as unique to us as a fingerprint. Every person on the planet is living in a world of their choosing, albeit unconsciously, created through the shit of judgments and beliefs, etc. But we have the power to change this completely once we realize how life works.

Three principles create our life experience. Just like the elements of chemistry create compounds. Like H_2O creates a compound of water, these "elements" produce the compounds that we experience as life. When you change the mixture, you change your life. This statement is descriptive rather than prescriptive, so knowing this is giving you the freedom to create your life as you want it, by design rather than by default.

Three atoms make up a water molecule: two hydrogen and one oxygen. There are billions of molecules in just one drop of water. There are three states we see this compound take:

- Water is fluid and takes the shape of the vessel or surface that it's in contact with.

- Bruce Lee said, "Be water my friend,"[8] meaning to be versatile and adapt to your surroundings, or your opponent, which is usually life itself. We can adapt by being aware of our state in the moment.

- Ice is solid. It can be an awesome sight. Icebergs are often used in personal growth analogies to describe our conscious mind being the tip of the iceberg. The approximately one-tenth of the iceberg that's visible and our subconscious minds and all that's going on in there is the other 90 to 95 percent. The idea is that we are only aware of a small fraction of what is happening in our minds.

- Steam, or vapor, is the third state. This is in a sense formless, depending on the density, as it can be seen but doesn't usually have a form as such. Like a cloud that looks like you can walk on it, yet will not hold your weight, not that I've tried (I'm still a little tempted to try, though). I don't profess to be an expert on this subject so please accept this as an analogy, not as fact. But if you do walk on a cloud, please let me know what happens.

There are the three principles that create our experience of our life:

- The principle of Universal Mind, which is the intelligence behind all life.

- The principle of Universal Consciousness, the awareness that gives us experience (are you aware?)

- The principle of Universal Thought, the animator of life

So what?

Like forming a compound by mixing two or more elements, by combining mind, consciousness, and thought, you are creating your life in your unique way. This is the creation of what we experience, from the inside-out. Hence the expression of the inside out understanding.

When I first heard this, I thought it was a great concept. Okay, so there are three principles, big wow. I totally agreed with the idea, just was not really sold on the enormity of this understanding. Then I revisited it a few years later and was taught more deeply, or I heard it more deeply is probably a more accurate assessment. This time I took notice and went on with my usual compulsion to read everything and anything on the subject. Then, also in my usual manner, I got distracted by another shiny object and was obsessed with something else. Have you noticed that happen to you? It's a common trait to get close to breaking through, then we unconsciously sabotage our learning by getting distracted in some way.

This went on for quite a few years, so I won't bore you with any more of the details, but why I tell you that it was on and off is because it didn't click on the first, second, or maybe even third time around. I'm not talking about hearing it once on a podcast, I'm talking about immersing myself by reading dozens of books, listening to webinars, courses, even going to seminars that focused on this subject. The phrase that stuck in my mind is that we are living in the feeling of our thinking in the moment.

But it just wasn't gelling with me. Not because I didn't believe it, but because I didn't know what to do with it. In fact, it was upsetting, because I felt like I had lost my identity. "If it's all just thought, and there is no separation, who the hell am I?"

It's an Inside Job

I was introduced to the teachings of a person I never met but have grown to love—Sydney Banks. Originally from Scotland, he had moved to Canada and was known by his close friends as Scotty. As I learned from reading his work, he was looking for some guidance on improving his marriage. He wasn't obsessed like me in terms of reading everything he could get his hands on (plus it would be a lot harder to do so in those days), but he was searching in his own way.

He eventually went to a seminar on relationships. I say "eventually" because he canceled twice before eventually committing to going. I know that trait well. He was conversing with a fellow attendee who was a psychologist, telling Syd how insecure he, the psychologist, was. A psychologist, by the way, but hey, they're only human. Sydney Banks argued that no way was this guy as insecure as he was. A typical seminar conversation, but then Syd heard something that the psychologist casually said, but in a profound way, to Sydney Banks anyway.

The psychologist said, "You're not insecure, Syd. You just *think* you are."

This doesn't sound so profound to me, but Syd heard it at a much deeper level than just the words. Sydney Banks said to the psychologist, "Do you realize what you just said?"

"Of course I do, I don't make idle chatter," said the psychologist, getting a little defensive.

But Syd knew that he didn't because of his behavior toward him.

Sydney Banks's life paradigm began to change in that moment. (There's much more to this story but I don't want to butcher it. Please go to www.sydneybanks.org to get the full story. I highly recommend reading *The Enlightened Gardener*.[17])

This is so hard to comprehend, that a somewhat flippant comment could spark such a paradigm shift of seeing that everything was all made up of thought. Though I can sort of relate to how this could happen. I've experienced hearing something said or written maybe after the umpteenth time myself, and something suddenly clicked for me this time, even though I was hearing the same thing in the exact same way, I just heard it at a deeper level.

This, though, was a whole other level of life-changing for him; way beyond our imagination, I'm guessing.

This began his journey, and I highly recommend you look at the website www.sydneybanks.org to get the full story. This fascinating story helps us understand that it wasn't just a great insight or a great idea. This was an enlightening experience that few people in our history have ever had.

I, being me, was a skeptic of the inside-out understanding (the three principles) at first.

Not that I ever thought that he was a fraud, you can just sense the sincerity and his energy in his words. It was more like a feeling of familiarity; like it didn't teach me anything that I didn't know. I was practicing and teaching NLP (neurolinguistic programming) at the time.

So, when I first heard about this inside-out understanding, which again, the main phrase that sticks in my mind is that "we live in the feeling of our thinking 100 percent of the time, moment to moment," I thought that I agreed with it. I didn't realize how profound that statement was until many years later. I threw it in with the rest of my tools in my NLP toolbox, thinking it was the same as what I was already thinking and teaching.

I understood that these three principles were what made up our entire existence, experientially. I understood that, like H^2O makes the compound of water, the three principles mixed make up our compound experience of the world. I understood that we each have a separate experience as unique as our fingerprints.

So, when we think of reality, we are only seeing our subjective, perceptive reality and thinking that it's the truth. We take the objective situation, relate it to ourselves subjectively, and then create a belief that seems like an objective observation.

Let's say you went to New York and had a wonderful time. The hotel was amazing, and the people couldn't do enough for you. The weather was like you were in Hawaii and just made everything perfect. You would think of New York and presume that the reality is that New York is (or at least can be) a magical place, well worth visiting.

I go to New York, get mugged on the subway, end up having a horrible time, and vow never to go back in my lifetime. And it's freaking freezing there! And the cab drivers rip you off! It's a place you should never go to. (I'm not saying this is true, New Yorkers ☺)

We do this unconsciously and "know," as in believe that it's a fact.

We fall into the illusion that what we experience is reality, when the truth is that it's our subjective reality, made up from our conception of the three principles. We cannot see the principles, just like we cannot see the individual molecules of H_2O, we can only see the principles in action, just like we can see ice, steam, and water.

This is so much more powerful than the usual tactics on "how to pretend you don't have anxiety."

You may have heard of the story of the indigenous people who hadn't ever seen ships before the explorers, led by Captain Cook, came to their island. It was reported by Captain Cook that while the locals greeted the small landing boats, they couldn't see the ships moored offshore, even though they were looking right at them. Joseph Banks recorded in his diary that the fishermen were so oblivious to this huge ship passing right by them that they carried on without even glancing in its direction. It seems ridiculous, but it was not in their conscious reality, so they did not experience it.[26] Our eyes are like projectors rather than camera lenses. We are not seeing the world with our eyes, we are seeing the many filters (mainly shit) that we have in place where the information goes through, which is then internalized as fact.

I somewhat understood it but did not actually realize it, big difference. This is the only reality that we know. We are living in the thought, and that thought has a feeling attached, like two sides of a coin. It's not just a case of seeing this floating image in front of us and deciding not to engage with it; we're engaged! We must allow the illusion to gradually break down through a deep understanding that it's not real, it's our shit-stained reality.

So, let's say this reality of ours is not what we want. (Obviously, if it is what you want, then enjoy.) If it's not a situation that we want to stay in, at this point it's the equivalent of H_2O in the ice state, we have hardened it with our filtered attention. It's hard to try and move that stuff around, let alone mold it, once it's hardened. Water or steam can be molded easily in comparison, but when we try to mold this very well-formed ice (not sculpt, mold), it's exhausting and fruitless, as I can attest to. It's like trying to turn a chair back into a tree.

This is where the realization comes into effect. If we didn't know about how H_2O changes to other states, we would continue to struggle to move the ice in its condition, like trying to change a situation with tactics and strategies. But knowing that if we heat the ice, it turns to water, and eventually to steam or vapor, we can very easily use this knowledge to move or use this H_2O to our advantage.

When we realize that we are living in the feeling of our thinking, not the feeling of the world, then we understand that to try to change a situation is like trying to remold the shape of ice. But if we let go of the hold, it's the equivalent of heating that ice, first to water, so we become more fluid and see a bigger picture and new perspectives, then to vapor, where we allow the feelings to evaporate, and what is left is simply vaporized energy, which is easily moved. In fact, it naturally rises to a better feeling state.

When we're living in the block of ice without this understanding, and some dick like me tells you to just breathe and let go, that's tough because it doesn't seem possible for this stuff to clear by itself. We think we've got to do the hard work and keep smashing and molding and fixing. "What doesn't kill you makes you stronger." That might work on the physical, horizontal way of thinking, maybe to build physical strength, but makes no sense when you see the principles, the flexibility, and changeability of H_2O, rather than the ice.

If we believe the world is like ice, then we need to fix our broken self-esteem. We need to get better at communicating and "man up," regardless of our gender, to face our fears head-on and understand that the struggle is real. Yes, it's real, frozen in your fingerprint version of the principles. But when you start to realize the truth, it's insane to try to create your life this way. It's not impossible, because some people somehow struggle through it, but it's certainly not the best option and definitely not my choice.

How do we heat up this ice to remold it, then?

We stop resistance to it and we welcome the feeling with awareness. Not the situation, remember, because that's heavily tainted by our shit judgments. We allow the feelings, then we go into a state of awareness. This can be opening your vision into peripheral vision, which we will do in the exercise section, or simply noticing your breathing or the feeling of your body, part by part. Remember it's not the strategies but the intention that counts, so please don't get too hung up on what to do. You're not trying to "do awareness." Awareness is simply being aware.

Of what though? Of everything and anything, without judgment. Letting go of the judgment is the magic key.

When we witness our feelings without judgment, we are letting go of the hold of the feelings and just feeling. This is like heating the ice, and it slowly melts. We stay in awareness, taking our attention from the feelings and into the moment.

I will go through this with you again, so just relax and read. It's the habit of doing that gets us thinking we need to remember this or start doing something. This is freezing the situation while missing the core message. As you read this, you are starting to realize the truth, and the truth will set you free.

I love the simple exercise that Hale Dwoskin, author of *The Sedona Method*,[27] gives. He says to place a pen in your hand. Now squeeze your hand shut and hold as tight as you can. Notice how much energy it takes to keep holding that pen tightly. Now turn your hand over so you are still holding the pen, but loosely, with your fingers down, gently keeping it from falling to the ground. Now let the pen go.

How was it? Did you find it hard to let go? Of course not, it's easy. Do you feel less tension now you are not struggling to squeeze the pen?

As simple as that exercise is, it's a fantastic example of what we do with our thoughts and feelings. We hold on for dear life and waste a ton of energy, not realizing that we are the ones who are putting the pressure on ourselves unnecessarily.

You just let go.

The obvious and common reaction to this is that it can't be that easy. And I say . . . No, it's not. Why? Because a belief is not tangible; you cannot hold it in your hand.

But what you can hold is tension in the body when a thought or belief (which is a thought that you keep thinking) comes into your mind. So rather than struggling to let go of the thought/ belief, you focus on letting go of the tension in your body, allowing your body to relax and dispersing the stressful chemicals that are emitted due to the trigger caused by the belief.

It may take practice. I would be so bold as to say it absolutely will. Some people have been known to get it immediately, but that wasn't me. Most people need at least some practice, if not a lot of practice, like I did. Start simply with something easy by letting go of the idiot that pushed in front of you in traffic. No positive thinking, no affirmations or reframing, just picture the thoughts and feelings as a pen, and let go of all the tension. Go through your body, relaxing the shoulders, the face, etc., going through the whole body, but quickly. This need not take more than a few seconds once you are used to it. Do this as often as you can. It never hurts to be constantly relaxing the body, just the noticing will be heating up that ice anyway, I promise you.

Wha?

- Three principles create our life experience: mind, consciousness, and thought. Like the three elements of two hydrogens and one oxygen make water, these three elements make a compound called our life experience. Every one of us mixes our own unique compound. This is a fundamental misunderstanding, but now you are aware that you can be a deliberate creator of your own life.

- Like ice and steam are very different to handle, the life compounds we create can also be very different to handle. The shit can get hardened so it's hard to get rid of.

- By letting go, we heat the compound and make it easier to create the life we want.

- Practice letting go, just like letting go of a pen. Letting go of judgment and the tension in your body will transform your life.

Let's Practice:

Think of a situation that you want to let go of, really focus all your attention on it, on all the shit. Sometimes this alone starts to heat it up by bringing awareness. Now notice the tension that comes as a result in the body. Let go of the judgment and pay attention to the feeling.

Breathe in, hold for a second, and as you exhale allow yourself to let go and feel the hold of that situation release. Notice how you feel, without judgment of that feeling.

Focus on one point in the room, then, without losing your attention on this point, expand your vision to see as far right as you can, then, without losing vision of the point and the right, look as far left as you can, without moving the eyes, just expanding your vision. Now look to the ceiling or as high as you can, again not losing the awareness of the point, which may be a little blurry by now but keep your attention to it and left and right. Now look as far down to the floor as you can while maintaining all other areas, eyes fixed. This is putting you into peripheral vision. Notice how you feel.

Now drop into seeing from the back of your eyes, like you're looking at your eyes looking out. You won't see your eyes, but just have that awareness of seeing behind your eyes, like you've softened your eyes. Practice this for a few minutes each day, more if you're inclined to do so, as the more you do this, the more you will start to get awareness. It seems like hard work at first, but the more you do this you will find yourself in this awareness almost immediately without needing to open your vision as it becomes second nature.

Think of a situation that you are struggling with, you can start with something trivial to begin, just so that you can practice efficiently. Don't go trying to fix the problem of a lifetime on your first try. Notice the feelings associated with this situation. If appropriate (this is not a good idea in public), say the feelings out loud. This is not essential, so just notice them if that is easier. Open your awareness by looking through but behind the eyes. Now, allow the feelings in your body, without resistance, welcome them, remember you are not saying that you want to feel this way, you are simply letting go of the resistance to them, keeping your awareness behind the eyes. Stay in awareness if possible. Notice how you feel, and repeat as necessary.

Practice makes perfect. Don't wait for the shit to hit the fan and then say that this doesn't work. Practice at least daily, if not several times daily, so that when the big challenges come up you will be ready and able.

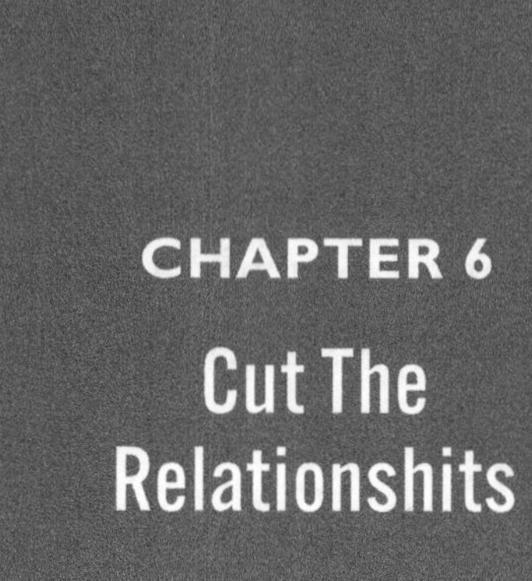

*"It's not you that people like or dislike
it's what they make up in their heads,
or what you make up in your head
about what they're thinking."*

LEE VALLELY

We think, right? But then we start thinking about the thinking, then thinking about the thinking about the thinking. Before we know it, we are in a completely different world than what we were originally experiencing. When we are in a conversation with someone, we are not seeing that person, we are seeing our mass of thinking about that person, whether we know them or not.

Within seconds of meeting someone, we have made an educated guess about them based on how they dress and how confident, friendly, or attractive they are. We can't help ourselves; it's built into our system.

We have also made up a mass of thinking about ourselves, so we're not even seeing ourselves, but thinking about our thinking about thinking about ourselves. There's a great quote from Charles

Cooley: "I am not what you think I am. I am not what I think I am. I am, what I think, you think I am."[28]

See the person with consciousness just above? This is when we're in the present, before thought, just being in nature or just in the world, fully present. Then we have a thought about what we're experiencing, thinking. Then we go above the line on the drawing, conjuring up more thinking, judging, and creating so much information that our minds can be in a seemingly perpetual state of overwhelm.

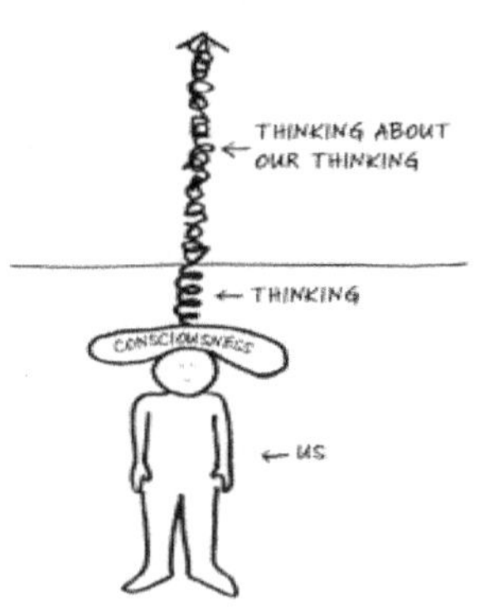

This is what happens when we are creating people in our mind. The person we've created is not even close to the real person, but rather a made-up concept of what we believe this person to be. Even if we know this person very intimately, this is still the case, because we are still making assumptions about this person. So, when we are interacting, whether with a person we know or have just met, our made-up person is interacting with their made-up person, so neither is talking to a real person.

Confusing? This is almost every interaction on the planet if the people are in their heads.

But when we speak and interact from the heart, our heart is interacting with their heart. This is a pure conversation, without any shit interfering. It's never in the words. You don't need to practice a script. Just come from the heart.

Let's talk about how.

Let Your Other Brain (Heart) Do the Thinking

It's normal at this point to want some great strategies and exercises that will get us to connect from the heart as opposed to the head, and then we can practice until they are a habit. I have done this my entire adult life, but we must be careful.

I heard a story about a guy who joined the police force. He was incredibly keen; he took everything they taught him and went to the extreme to practice and master it daily (I can relate). He was in one demonstration where he would be attacked by a gunman (his training partner), and he was shown how to disarm the assailant and take his gun. So, as his partner would pull the gun on him, he would immediately twist the gun from his hand and turn the gun back on him, then hand it back to his partner and go again.

He practiced, for hours, for days. He would twist the gun from his partners hands, and hand it back to him, twist the gun from his hands, and hand it back to him. He became so proficient after hours and hours of practice that it was second nature.

One day as he was on the beat, a real assailant pulled a gun on him. Luckily, he was so well practiced, he, with precision, twisted the gun from the assailant's hands and turned it back on him. . . then gave the gun back to the assailant![29]

True story

Okay, I don't know if it's 100 percent true, but it shows that, in theory, it looks great to practice scenarios, using "if, then" strategies, and you may feel that this is a great way to be able to deal with a social situation, and I do appreciate that sometimes they can help, but a lot of times it can be so obvious and off-putting, because you metaphorically hand them back the gun. *Strategies will never be better than you being authentically yourself.* Get that part down initially before looking for tactics.

The other part about strategies and tactics, and the reason I am not a fan of them, initially, is that they tend to get you out of your heart and into your shithead too much. Which, if you tend to get anxious, is the last place you want to go.

If you want to connect with a person, whether that be intimately, or simply meeting a new friend or business associate, the person must feel that you are present. How can you be present when you are thinking about your next move or whether you said that last statement correctly or not? Trust me I'm speaking from experience here.

This is possibly the most important information that you will ever hear about relationships and your life, because relationships create your life, so don't make them relationshits.

The most interesting person is the most interested person.

You become the most interesting person to the person in front of you when you are interested in the person in front of you. I'm not talking about drooling over them, I mean really interested. Not fake interested, not a tactic from the shit head to get them to like you, truly interested.

How the heck do you do that?

Get out of your own way; basically, the opposite of having lines and strategies in your head. Be curious, lighthearted, and most importantly, free of any expectation.

People don't care what you know until they know that you care, as the saying goes. Talk and listen from the heart and you will connect with anyone at a much deeper level than you may have ever experienced.

I used to facilitate mental wellness groups in a treatment center, with people with addictions and some with mental disorders and dual diagnoses. I attended my classes fully armed with facts and figures and solutions to their problems. I worked my arse off. I wanted to blind them with science so they would be awestruck by the information that I had presented, and they could instantly transform their lives.

I worked roughly four hours for every hour that I facilitated and had ten-plus classes a week. With the same people too, so I couldn't simply replicate. That didn't include the previous studies, constant reading and studying, and preparation I had done. I'm exhausted just thinking about it.

Andi, my wife, did two groups a week at the same place. She had a different approach than me. Andi did zero preparation for her class, rarely read anything much (she did through osmosis because I was forever reading and watching stuff), and just showed up. I thought she was insane!

When my class was finished, people would walk out saying that it was good. Good?! I worked my ass off; it should've been life-changing!

I saw people on many, many occasions come out of Andi's class almost spellbound. They would say that it was an amazing class. WTF!? She never did any prep. She had no clue even what the subject was; she would just waltz in like Lady Muck.

I had to know what her secret was. So, I decided to take part in one of her groups (alongside my uncle who also is an incredible group facilitator). We couldn't make sense of what she was saying! "All you need is love, love is all you need," something like that.

We left totally confused, but realized why her classes were so popular. She had no agenda, just a deep interest in the participants' well-being and an energy that lifted everyone else in the room.

I hadn't studied for that!

I finally realized that what reaches people is not just what you say, even how you say it, it's how present you feel while you are with them. I was thinking about what I was going to say next. She was present with them, nothing but them on her mind, listening and speaking from the heart.

We can argue (and I did) that they needed to learn how to improve their lives and get out of bad habits of thought, and that's somewhat true.

First, they needed to know that they were okay, that they were loved, and that was okay to feel good and feel good about themselves, and to feel that you are present and you care about them. When we adopt this principle into every interaction we have, from the love of our life to the person loading our groceries, a miracle will happen before your eyes on a daily, if not hourly, basis.

This is not easy. It wasn't for me, anyway. It takes practice . . . a lot of practice. But what could be more important than being phenomenal at connecting with people?

Want to earn more money? Learn this.

Want to find the love of your life? Learn this.

Want to improve your relationshits that you have? Learn this.

Want to have more, better friends? Learn this.

My reluctance to just showing up came from the fear of being taken advantage of, especially doing groups, as they were tough cookies and I was afraid that they might think I was a pushover. But, as I will discuss in the next chapter, there's a big difference between appreciating and loving people and allowing them to walk over you. That's people-pleasing, which is totally different and stuck in the shit. I'm talking about connecting.

There was a story about a lady way back in the UK who had the privilege of meeting the two main candidates for office at the time, Benjamin Disraeli and William Gladstone. (I told you it was way back.) The reporters asked her the big question: "Who was your favorite?"

She replied that when in conversation with Gladstone, she was convinced that he was the most talented, learned, generous, and accomplished person that she had ever had the privilege of speaking to. Pretty impressive.

When she was in the company of Disraeli, however, she was convinced that she was the most talented, learned, generous, and accomplished person that he had ever had the privilege of listening to. Who do you think was her favorite?[30]

When we come from the heart, we let go of judgments of ourselves and others, the barriers between us melt away, and we are completely at ease in each other's company. We are home.

Now what?

- Notice life without judgment.

- Speak and listen from the heart, not the shithead. Don't fall into tactics and end up giving the gun back.

- We all live in a separate world, so it's not about you, it's about your connection.

- Just be. Be with the person you are with, be with the situation you are in, be with you.Relax, and know that your life is changing for the better. Don't be happy when . . . Be happy now!

Let's work the shit out of you:

I want to make sure that you understand that this is a practice., It is not essential for every encounter, so please don't get freaked out if you don't have time to do this. The best time to practice this is always.

Find a place where you will not be disturbed for five minutes or so. Once you have practiced this a few times, you can do this anywhere and within seconds.

Close your eyes if appropriate to do so. Place your hands on your heart and breathe in and out through the nose. Imagine you are breathing into your heart. Now imagine connecting to a white light above you, maybe 300 feet up in the sky. Connect to this white beam of light and let it shoot down into your body through the crown of your head, down to your feet, and into the center of the earth. Now the beam mixes with the fire of the Earth's core shoots back up through your body and merges with every cell of your body. You are on fire!!! In a good way, of course. Let this beautiful energy surround you, giving a 360-degree beam of light. Now open your eyes, allowing this fire inside of you to light up your present moment with energy. Knowing that this energy will allow you to simply be in the present moment, focusing on the people who you are meeting and conversing with, while you are perfectly aligned with universal energy coursing through your veins.

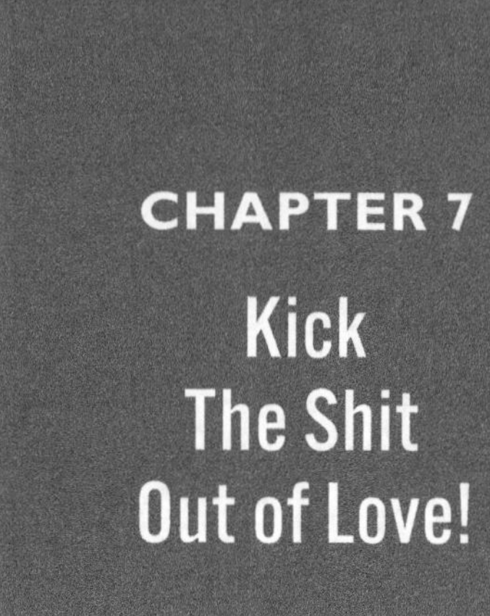

*"If you could look inside the heart
of any and every single human being,
you would fall in love
with them completely."*[31]

MOOJI

I used to cringe when people used the word "love"—partly because I was being righteous and judgmental of their use of the word (in my head luckily, not out loud). I felt that people threw the word around but had no clue what it meant. The idea of love was in almost every book I read, telling me, "The answer is Love, insert question." Blah blah, bloody blah.

My question was, HOW?!

I understood (intellectually) the concept of unconditional love, forgiveness, and compassion for everyone. It just seemed weak and so daunting a task that, as you can gather by now, I did a lot of thinking about this. I would cringe every time someone puked out that damn word.

Then there was this guy named Derrick Mason on a 3PGC (three principles global community) Zoom call. This is a guy who went through way more than me in his life, yet there he was spitting out this cuss word "Love" in every sentence. But what was amazing was that there was no resistance to his words. He was speaking from the heart, and what's more is that I believed him, 100 percent.

I didn't even believe myself when I would say it, yet here is an ex-con, by his own admission, not pushing the word in people's faces, but feeling and meaning what he's saying!? This blew my mind. Not because he was an ex-con and "isn't that great that he's a changed man," but because of his sincerity and his beautiful energy.

I have heard hundreds of very well-known and respected people speak about this, but he wasn't trying to impress or even teach. He was talking about his life and how he felt. I couldn't help but feel love for him. I highly recommend that you listen to his story on the website www.beyond-recovery.co.uk.[32]

So, what was my excuse?

No Love Please, I'm British

I knew I couldn't just go out and be a love bug instantaneously. So, the magic formula was put into action. I simply noticed how I reacted and what my thoughts or feelings were in situations, without judging them. This is what I have found. Eventually, noticing without judgment becomes love. That beautiful soul, Sydney Banks already said it: "When you take away all interference, what's left is love."[17]

When you see life through the eyes of love (OMG, I'm sounding like the crazies now), people, circumstances, and perceptions change before your very eyes.

Like most things in life, it's not instantaneous. There are going to be (many) moments when you are determined to see through your loving eyes and then some dick, er I mean person, is horrible to you, or worse . . . They cut you off in traffic the mother . . . loving souls that they are.

This can easily push you straight off course, but it's not the situation that disrupts you. If you simply notice (after a few chosen words and possibly a hand signal or two) that you are not seeing through loving eyes right now, you can simply return to practicing, or rather being, that person, seeing through the eyes of love as much as you can. If the word "love" is too much, replace it with "appreciation." The energy vibration is the same. This is what I did when I started. If you have just a little more appreciation than you did before, you are heading in the right direction, and then, like compound interest, as you keep noticing and appreciating, this little appreciation will turn into a life transformation.

I really do mean transformational, because it is the key to a life free of anxiety and fear.

It's going to feel unnatural at first because we think we must be a certain way or say things like a princess would. But it's just a feeling; the words and actions will take care of themselves. Add this to the mix of being naturally interested in the person or situation that's in front of you, and you have a beautiful recipe for having the life that you have always wanted.

An amazing speaker and author with the best name ever, Zig Ziglar, had an affirmation for people to remember. He said, "You can have everything in life that you want, if you help enough other people get what they want."[33]

That's a great metaphor for life and covers everything. So, what do people want?! A Rolls Royce? A beach house? A body like Kate Beckinsale? Okay, this is my list, but what people truly want is not things; it's what they think the things will give them. People want to feel accepted, to be loved, to be appreciated, and to be happy.

That's what you can give to people simply by having a sense of seeing through loving eyes, being interested, and having non-judgment in your heart. I know it's a challenge, but you can have everything in life you want by learning to get out of your own way so that these natural feelings come through. Because you are a resource, overflowing with high vibrations.

It seems like hard work, yet we are the ones making it hard for ourselves. Remember, negative emotions are not natural, even though they feel "normal." They also take a huge effort and energy to maintain, which is why most people are exhausted, holding down the metaphorical beachball of wellbeing under the water of negative thinking, alias the matrix, not realizing that it's not our natural state and we just need to let go. Then it pops up to the surface of our conscious awareness without any effort. I could (and possibly will) write a book on this one subject alone. Just realize that it is not in the doing that the miracles happen, and they will happen once you realize that it's in the being, seeing, and noticing.

So, the big question that is usually asked of me at this point is, if you go around with love in your eyes and no judgment, won't every Tom, Dick (especially Dick), and Harriet take advantage? Won't people just walk all over you?

YES, if you're an ASS . . . but not if you're ASSertive (see what I did there?), which we will discover in the next chapter.

Let Go of Your Shit Attachments

In his incredible book *You Can Have It All*,[34] Arnold Patent said, "We don't create abundance. Abundance is always present. We create limitations."

I would add that the same is true with relationships and even our health. We create our limitations by attaching to them. We have the power of free will. It's so powerful that we have the capacity to enslave ourselves.

Does that seem a bit strong? Let me ask you: are you attached to your spouse or significant other, if you have one? If you say you are, then you are enslaving not only yourself, but the other person, too. If you love someone, set them free.

Are you attached to your kids if you have any? What family are you attached to? You have enslaved them, and yourself, if you are. Oh, these are fighting words I know, but it's true.

We have heard countless stories of people who would have loved to have been artists or actors, etc., who were forced to take a more traditional career path, if not monetarily, simply by well-meaning parents who wanted the best for them and were afraid that they were not capable of making the right decision for themselves. We all know that's true, and we would never be guilty of such a thing . . . right?

But there's another side to this that is not so obvious to self, yet sometimes blatantly obvious to others. Moreso today than ever before, I think that kids (and you make your own mind up as to when that label ends as there are "kids" who still live at home in their thirties) are wrapped up in cotton wool and given everything, so they never have to fend for themselves, think for themselves, or learn by themselves. We think that if they get a good education that the rest doesn't matter, because they will be able to get a good job, etc.

This illusion has its merits. But the trouble starts when they don't even have basic awareness and the capabilities of thinking for themselves or coping by themselves. This enslaves that child, so they become dependent. When you are attached, you are influencing their wisdom. Or rather, blocking their wisdom, believing that you are more aware than their own wisdom and creating strings attached to everything.

Does this mean that you must stop caring? Yes! But wait it's not what you think.

You have love and compassion, so the natural caring is automatic, but if you "care" in the more commonly thought of way, that's trying to take care of them, being attached to them and what they do, rather than caring for them.

When we care in the physical sense, we usually mean we're concerned for them, worrying, afraid of what might happen. That's attachment and the belief that they are not capable of thinking for themselves. Therefore, people can get things like "empty nest syndrome" and a broken heart. They have attached their identity to their kids, family, or partner, rather than allowing their family or partner to find their own identity, leading to anxiety and disappointment for pretty much everyone concerned.

If you weren't attached, you would be even more in love with your significant other, your kids, friends, family, your world, house, job, the list could go on forever.

I know this sounds cold, but I promise you it's the most loving thing that you can do. There's no better feeling than being loved unconditionally, without judgment or attachments. And there's no better feeling than loving unconditionally.

Unconditional love is the antidote to fear and anxiety.

When you can begin to see the magic of unconditional love throughout your life, everyone in your family, and in your presence, will feel more loved and cared for than they ever felt in their lives, even more than when you did everything for them.

For many years we worked in treatment centers with "kids" in their twenties and thirties, mostly. There were many horror stories of what people went through in their lives. Surprisingly, the biggest complaint from kids coming from a more "normal" upbringing was that their parents or guardians gave them complete freedom. They got whatever they wanted and knew how to manipulate them. You would think that the kids would appreciate this, but most were angry at their parents because they felt that the lack of guidance gave them a lack of self-discipline, causing their own demise. You might think that this shows that the family was not attached, but the reality is that the family were so attached to the kids that they wanted to do everything that they could to make them happy, but creating the opposite effect as the kids were not able to rely on their own wisdom.

What does unconditional love have to do with non-attachment? When you take away the interference, the attachments to what people do, say, and act in life, the judgments both good and bad (of course I'm talking on a subconscious level, I'm not saying don't be proud of your kids), what's left is pure, "unadulterated," unconditional love; one of the most powerful energies in the universe. Correction: the energy that creates the universe.

Imagine giving that gift to the ones you love the most.

This makes you (not really, but it seems like it) God-like, but amongst Gods. Every one of us has this ability, this energy, this potential because we are a part of God (change the word if it upsets you, please use whatever resonates with you).

Like a drop of water from the ocean, if you let that drop go back into the ocean, it's indistinguishable from any other part of the ocean. Yet when you simply look at the drop by itself, you would be forgiven for not seeing its magnificence as part of the mighty force and beauty of the ocean. This is a metaphor, and it doesn't do justice to the magnificence of you and everyone you meet.

You are the Universe, God, higher power, whatever word works best for you. You have that wisdom, that knowledge, that power, that magnificence within you. The only reason that you, me, and pretty much every person on the planet doesn't know and use this gift is because it is clouded over by thoughts, beliefs (which are a cluster of thoughts), and by interference in its many shapes and sizes of shit. Remember: we see ourselves as separate, the drop of water, rather than a part of the entire ocean. If you really saw that we are all connected, then do you think that you might treat people differently? Competition would fall away.

I'm not talking about sports, because of course that's (mostly) healthy competition; I'm talking about the backstabbing, jealousy, or feelings of superiority or inferiority. You are no less, or no more, important than any other person on the planet.

Potential - interference = performance

You Are a Genius

Oh, if only you (and I) could just hear this and think "okay" and then go ahead and listen to our own wisdom, our genius. Because, please hear this, you are a genius, you just don't KNOW it (although some egotistical people might think they do) yet. If we could hear that on an experiential, rather than intellectual, level, we would all be geniuses because it's already within us.

I remember being on an NLP master practitioner course with the amazing Richard Bandler[35] (who, by the way, has not only co-created one of the most well-known and successful psychological therapies, but is also a published best-selling author many times and has composed countless pieces of music. So, he's certainly tapping into some genius somewhere). He got about five people to come on stage as he was recording this session for a documentary. They were asked whether they believed that they were artistic or not. (I was picked to go up, but someone got up in my place by mistake and I didn't want to embarrass him, so I missed my chance).

He chose people purposely who said that they were not artistic. Each person that was on stage had a story about why they felt that they could not be artistic. Each one had been told by different teachers, parents, or guardians that they were not gifted with this talent. I myself had this experience, so for my entire life I doubted my own abilities. I was even taught to become right-handed when I was clearly left-handed.

These people were put under hypnosis by the man who was voted as the number one hypnotist on the planet. Pretty good deal, hey. That's why I wanted to get up there. After being in hypnosis, they were given the suggestion to paint, draw, or write a poem, or to do something else creative that appealed to them. Each one did beautiful work.

Were they masterpieces? Well, no, because they had only just allowed themselves to be open to this idea. So, just like the baby learning to walk, or the child learning to ride a bike, the potential is there, but there is still a little practice needed to allow that genius to come through. But they were all good.

Seeing this completely changed my way of thinking.

I'm reminded of the fable of the lion cub who was adopted by sheep when his mother was killed. The cub, unaware of his history, always admired the lions and wished he could be one, but the other sheep made fun of him and told him not to think such crazy thoughts, "those lions are so powerful, and we are so weak," they would say.

One day the herd of sheep was alerted because a pride of lions was coming. The sheep bleated, or whatever they do, and tried to scatter and hide. The one lion spotted this lion cub shivering in a corner bleating to please spare his life. The lion roared, "Come with me!"

The cub did what he was told, and the lion took him to a pond.

"Look down in the pond, what do you see?!"

The cub gasped and jumped back, as he saw a lion in the reflection.

"You are not a sheep. You are a lion!"[36]

Of course, this is the abbreviated version, but you get the picture.

The reason I tell this old story is because of a misunderstanding I had with the message. (Or, that the message has changed for me, as I don't truly know what the message was for the author.) The message I used to believe was that I was a lion, stuck with the societal sheep who just followed the crowd. I always felt that I was something more, that I was better than the sheep life. This was great when I was in the "break-down-walls, lunch-is-for-wimps" attitude. Other times I would feel that maybe I was a sheep, maybe I should know and accept my limitations. Later though, I realized that we are all one, we are all magnificent beings, we are all a part of God (universe, higher power). So, initially, this metaphorical tale was a more egotistical "you can do it" type of story.

But then there was a realization, I think I heard it retold by Michael Neill, a phenomenal speaker and author of many books, as I mentioned before.

The new (in my mind) metaphor is that the sheep are not the animal, but a representation of the many of us asleep in the matrix. We all have this ability in life within us, but we're under the hypnosis of the outside, egotistical world. As sheep we believe that it's only what we experience with our five senses that is real, everything else is out of our control. We wish we could fix ourselves to be the lion, but we accept our limitations. After all, how could we possibly be lions when all we have is this sheepish body and little brains? The lions were just lucky I guess (good luck, bad luck, who knows).

The lions come along, and we fear them, admire them, are envious of them. But the one lion who is awake takes us and shows us that we, too, are lions. We are all lions. We are the ocean, believing we're just a drop of water. I want to repeat this, we are ALL lions, we just don't know it yet.

This made all the difference. This made sense as to why we doubt ourselves when others can easily see the potential staring us in the face. This shows why there's so much anxiety and depression because people cannot "find" themselves. I was lost, but now I'm found.

One of the biggest questions people tend to ask is, "What is my purpose?" We are all searching for something that we already have and a place that we are already in. This is our purpose: to wake up to be the lion that we always have been.

Do What Now?

- Love doesn't come from others; it comes from within. It is abundant. You don't give or receive love, you are love.

- Non-attachment creates a loving connection, even though we have been taught the opposite. Non-attachment does not mean that you don't care; that's indifference. Non-attachment means that you are not attached to the story. You see the diamond in them, as well as in yourself.

- Empathy is exhausting, fully attached, and sometimes debilitating. Compassion allows caring without attachment, and a knowing that they are going to be okay.

- The more we let go of attachment to things being a certain way, the more we get into the flow and feel Love.

- **Love your practice. Practice your love** 🤍

This meditation will help to embody this way of thinking. Remember you can download this at: www.shifthappens.global/bookdownloads

Here's something to do as often as you can remember to do it:

As you breathe in, imagine you are breathing in Love, into your heart, and then this love energy is penetrating every cell in your body. As you breathe out, imagine breathing out all that overflowing love (appreciation, abundance) into the world around you, creating a beautiful loving feeling for yourself and everyone who comes into contact with you. Once you have established this as a personal ritual, you can simply breathe in "Loved" and breathe out "Loving," which will create the feeling of this overflowing love and abundance that you can't help but want to give away to others, as you cannot possibly keep it all to yourself. You will be experiencing this feeling with every breath you take and giving this energy out with every breath you exhale.

Again, remember to change the word if you feel resistance, the key here is to let go of all resistance, especially judgment.

CHAPTER 8

Don't Be an Ass, Be Assertive

I wanted to live life listening and connecting to wisdom as much as possible. I used to wait for wisdom to tell me what to do next, and then realized that I had to actually go do something for wisdom to kick in, in a sense. A little like the GPS where, until you move, it can't help you. So, I realized it was like the warmer / colder game and started to listen for the feelings and maybe voices, telling me if I was on track or not. I would keep reminding myself over and over, "I'm listening to my wisdom, I am feeling my wisdom, my wisdom is guiding me."

I didn't do them like affirmations, I just kept reminding myself that I was guided, that I didn't have to rely on myself. I had my own GPS. Was I warmer as in listening, or was I colder, as in ignoring or stressing?

Here's my revelation, I realized that I am not guided by wisdom, I do not have 100 percent access 24/7 to my wisdom, I am not talking to God/universe/higher self.

I am Wisdom, I am God, I am the GPS. The drop of the ocean.

It's not my wisdom. I am wisdom, it's me! The big I, rather than the egotistical i.

I never trusted "me" because I believed the real me to be the sheep, and the higher self to be the lion.

It still takes practice, learning which voice is the shit ego and which is my true voice: the diamond GPS.

One thing I've always been sure of is that when it's a voice telling me something, it's more likely to be the ego. When it's a sick or uncomfortable feeling, it's more likely to be the ego, at least for me. When its impulsive, even in a good way, it's usually ego.

When it's a knowing, I just know. Not negative or positive, just a deep knowing. That's the GPS.

I can't tell you why, I can't even say how I know. I don't know if it's a feeling, a vision, or a voice. I just don't know how, but I know.

There is no question about whether this is wisdom coming through.

Have you ever had that? It's crazy but it's true. I bet everyone on the planet has at some time experienced this knowing. This is something I can rely on. Why? Not because it's my wisdom talking to me, not because I got this strong emotion that wisdom is nudging me to go there or do this, but because it's me, behind the mask, knowing what to do in that moment.

It doesn't happen to me all the time, even though I've made it my life's work to walk, talk, and live as myself as much as heavenly possible. I know the idea is controversial, but if it resonates with you, try it on for size.

For me initially, the idea was way too egotistical, and I feared I might feel like I was better than others, feeling like I could do something that they couldn't. Like I was the lion 🦁 among sheep. But it's the complete opposite. We are all a part of the ocean; we all have our inner GPS.

We find compassion for others rather than sympathy, as sympathy tends to be based in the ego. Sympathy is looking at someone and feeling sorry for their situation being worse than yours. On the surface it seems like a nice thing to do, but unconsciously you are putting yourself onto a pedestal. You are saying that your life is better than theirs, otherwise, why would you feel sympathy?

Compassion is having unconditional love for that person, acknowledging and accepting what they're going through, yet always knowing that they are okay.

Knowing that they are not sheep having a hard life, they are a lion who hasn't realized it yet. Not everyone is ready to be tapped on the shoulder and awakened, so with empathy or sympathy, you may want to shake them out of sleep for their own good, but you don't know what is for their own good.

With compassion, you can allow them to go at their own pace while being there for them when, and only when, they are ready. This is the beauty of not being attached, but compassionate and loving unconditionally.

This is where compassion is important. It is not our right or ability to tell people how to live their lives, or whether they are ready or not to be awakened. Like the good luck, bad luck farmer story. How do we know when and whether someone should be ready, what's right for them, or if they should even follow our way of thinking? This goes for everyone: spouse, partner, sibling, parent, child, absolutely everyone you have ever encountered in your life.

What I now know is that we all are okay no matter what. I'm not talking materialistically, or even physically, because of course there are atrocities going on in the world that I could never be comfortable letting happen in my vicinity without doing everything possible to help the situation.

I'm talking on a spiritual level, beyond the physical and beyond the psychological.

I believe there are lessons to be experienced in the physical and to be learned in the spiritual.

I am not 100 percent sure, but I am starting to think that the people who have gone through the most heinous of crimes and had unspeakable suffering in their lives may be the most highly developed spiritually. (Please understand that we're talking spiritually, because when we look physically, how can anyone go through such things and be unscathed, or in fact better? Yet spiritually our diamond is still intact and can learn from it.)

Think of any sport, or even a game online. When you reach a certain level, you are placed into harder and harder circumstances and opponents so that you progress.

This is hard for even me to grasp, and I'm writing this, so I can't imagine how you are feeling reading it.

But let's say this was true. It would not take away your personal feelings, obligation, and motivation to help and care for someone as much as physically possible. However, by having compassion (not empathy, which will completely exhaust you, as you are too attached), you would be able to help this person/people, with a sense that there is a light at the end of this dark tunnel that they went through, that they were okay and were going to be okay no matter what. You would not be attached to the situation; therefore, you would be in a clear mind. You cannot save a drowning person by metaphorically drowning yourself.

It's like the starfish story (which has been told at least a million times so I will do the abbreviated version). A boy was on the beach where thousands upon thousands of starfish had been washed up as far as the eye could see. This boy was throwing a starfish back into the water to save it when a man tapped him on the shoulder and said, "Son, save your breath, there are thousands of them, it won't make a difference." The boy thinks for a moment, picks up and throws another starfish into the water, and says to the man, "It made a difference to this one."[37]

There are many learnings from this I'm sure, but the one that is relevant to compassion for me is that if you were in empathy, it could destroy your ability to help even one starfish, because you would feel devastated and overwhelmed by the vastness of the problem. The attachment to the fate of the starfish left on the beach would prevent you from having the wisdom to take any action to help those starfish that you could help.

With compassion, which to me is the same energy as unconditional love, you can see that, although helping that one person or that situation is less than perfect, "it made a difference to that one." This is the difference between overwhelm, thinking about your thinking about the situation, and being in the moment, in your heart, knowing what the next loving, compassionate step is.

What's even more exciting to me is that we never know how far the ripples of what we do go out into this (pond) world of ours. When you drop a stone into a pond, the ripples can reach the end of the pond. It's not just the act, but the energy we send out into the world. I'm sure you've heard of the phrase, and maybe even seen the film *Pay it Forward*.[38] It became a cliche after a while but imagine how much deeper and wider the ripples went from the acts of kindness and paying it forward in the world as a consequence of that film.

I don't know about you, but if I'm thinking about how annoying this person is for taking so long to order, then find out that the reason was that they were paying for my order, then that would change my state. I would then feel like being in a very giving state, probably for the rest of the day. This is the magic of compassion, love, and peace. It doesn't have to be forced; you don't have to go paying for everyone else's Starbucks. Noticing your feelings without judgment and without attachment will bring you into these energy states over time.

Potential—Interference (judgment, fear, anxiety i.e., shit) = Performance

Remember that this is our "natural" state. Unfortunately, not our "normal" state.

We have been programmed to look for the exceptions and the troubles, etc., to be concerned about, and to attach to them. This gets translated as one bad situation equals all, or at least many. So, if we leave well enough alone and keep noticing, being the change that we wish to see in the world, then the world, in fact, and not just our habits, will improve.

Baby steps, I'm getting ahead of myself.

The more we leave alone and just live life with less and less judgment and less attachment, we see more and more love, peace, and harmony come into our lives. The best part of all is that we become comfortable in our skin (with less of it too, in my case), and have a natural calm, a sense of giving without attachment, and no feeling of scarcity. We are more giving of our time, energy, and material things with no reason to hold back. With no scarcity, we don't worry about being taken advantage of. We don't judge the fairness of a situation. Scarcity is a huge trait of our ego.

There was an exercise commonly used called the ultimatum game,[39] where a group of people are told that they would receive $1000 divided by themselves and an unknown person behind a screen. First, they were told that it would be split fifty-fifty, and 100 percent of the participants agreed to this. Then it got less for the person and more for the unknown person behind the screen. When the amount got to one hundred dollars for the study person and 900 dollars for the mystery person, most people refused to accept!? They would rather have nothing than let the other person get so much more than them because that just "wasn't fair."

Rationally, that makes no sense whatsoever! They would be one hundred dollars better off than before, regardless of what the other person got. What's crazy is that this was an imaginary person. There wasn't even a person behind the screen!

We are so ingrained with this belief of fairness that we cut off our nose to spite our face at times. It's tricky, I know, because sometimes it is unfair and we feel the need to correct an injustice. But being assertive is a win-win, not a win-lose situation, as we will discuss. When we are lovingly assertive, we bring into power the energy that creates our world and that gives you and everyone else everything that they need.

When we are not so attached to situations, we can make much more rational decisions; we can metaphorically see past the egoistic trees and notice the wood.

> *When you are no longer trying to win,*
> *you can see the solution for*
> *everyone involved. Num sayin?*
>
> LEE VALLELY

I love how freeing this way of looking at what being assertive is, compared to being aggressive or passive. It creates a natural feeling of well-being, along with abundance and love.

It's hard to pinpoint from an intellectual understanding. People tend to mistake assertiveness for aggressiveness, though it can even be mistaken for weakness or passivity.

Here's a simple explanation from so many great teachers:

Aggression speaks for itself in the way some of us approach life. Do you know someone who seems to be constantly in a battle with someone, or usually multiple people/situations?

The equation of aggression is **I win, you lose.**

Although not obvious, this can be a victim mentality.

This can be the obvious, arrogant, bully type, but can also be the person who has been taken advantage of in the past and wants to "assert" themselves so they will not make that mistake again, but unfortunately they tend to overdo it. This is the person that might jump down your throat at the slightest verbal comment that most people wouldn't even notice, or certainly wouldn't take offense to. Or they might fight you on every subject of conversation because they have to be right. It's hard to be around these people a lot of the time, but they feel like they can't help themselves, as they see it as protection. Although it may not be too obvious, it's a scarcity, fear-based thinking. The person is doubting their abilities to have wisdom without being vigilant 24/7, just in case someone sneaks through the barriers. This is a victim mentality, shown as a righteous response. They're attached to the idea of attacking when, or even in advance of, being attacked. This is often mistaken for "telling it how it is" and being blunt. While this may be confused with assertive, there's still an edge to it. Assertiveness is smooth; there's no barrier between you and the other person because you are working together on the situation. Aggression is not seeing that person as an ally but a threat. It's subtle, but as you practice or notice this in others, you will start to appreciate the magic of never needing to be aggressive . . . Yeah, I said it. Passionate yes, aggressive no. This is not suppressing feelings; this is creating the correct feelings without the illusion of attack thoughts.

Then there is the **passive.** The equation for passive is: **You win, I lose.**

This can be attractive as a response because it creates the victim mentality. The martyr card is played, and this person is shown to "help everyone, but never themselves." Subconsciously remember; they're not doing this purposely. They truly believe that they are being authentic.

This very often turns into becoming passive-aggressive almost always at some point. There is also the scarcity, fear-based thinking here, and the passive person eventually wants to stand up for themselves or get angry, but it shows up in a passive-aggressive way, laying on guilt toward the intended person, mistaking this as being assertive.

The passive at some stage may get so annoyed and fed up with being taken advantage of that they finally become aggressive. The metaphorical straw that broke the camel's back, they lose it over something trivial, and they then look like the bad guy or girl because, on the surface, their reaction was so over the top for such a trivial act. This creates a bind, and the passive person probably ends up apologizing and feeling bad, yet this unfairness builds up inside and escalates. Not a healthy state, in my opinion, and I should know because I went between passive and aggressive for most of my intellectual life. I wanted to keep the peace, then wanted to kill everyone. Okay not quite that dramatic, but it felt like it sometimes. On the surface, the person seems to not be too attached to people's injustice of them in whatever way. But the attachment is very much there under the surface, bubbling up and ready to overflow in whatever way that may manifest itself. This can be a mental or physical breakdown of some kind, or both. It can, if not addressed, lead to sickness, anxiety and/or depression.

Potential - interference = performance.

In both traits, there is huge interference, leading to less than adequate performance. They are both going away from the heart, away from the inner GPS, creating disharmony in body and mind. They are both a symptom of limiting beliefs. Aka shit!

Then we come to **assertiveness**. Or, as I like to call it, being **lovingly assertive**.

This is a very misunderstood quality, because often both the aggressive and passive believe that they are being assertive, mistaking the two to be the same.

The passive can believe that assertiveness means being aggressive, and that's not what they want, especially as it hasn't worked out too well for them in the past, with them ending up being labeled as the bad guy and going even more passive and apologetic because they feel guilty. Or it can go the other way, where aggressive people feel that being lovingly assertive is simply giving in and being weak and passive. Or they swear that they are assertive and that people just can't take it. Blaming others is the main focus of an aggressive person. The key here is that by being both passive and aggressive, you are attached to the situation and blinded by this connection.

But here's the equation for assertiveness: **I win, you win**. It's always a win-win when you are being assertive.

I was taught in Chinese martial arts that when an attacker comes toward you with force, you never meet force with force. Metaphorically, you turn the attacker to look in the same direction as you, so you are no longer looking at each other as enemies. You are both looking for a solution. The attachment is gone from the idea of right and wrong, and the focus is placed on finding an amicable solution.

That doesn't mean that you are passive. Instead, you take control of the situation and only use what force is necessary. This is a great metaphor for assertiveness because you look at what the other person wants. This obviously varies greatly depending on the situation. it may be a case of asking that person what they want (I am only giving an example here, as this most definitely does not apply in every case). By stepping metaphorically into their shoes and seeing through the other's eyes, rather than seeing them as an opponent, helps find a resolution where you have a win-win solution.

In an aggressive encounter, the aggressor must save face, so it is important to give them a way out or not show them up. Like a bully, you never want to try to show them up in any way, but instead allow them to back down while "saving face." You also know what you want, so the question is how can you both come out of this, at least not losing, but preferably by both getting what you want? I honestly have created many friends from people who initially tried to bully me.

This is an amazing transformation in how we communicate. It seems like hard work at first, and it is because we believe that we must work all this out intellectually, using tactics and strategies. The only work you really need to do is to remind yourself to be lovingly assertive and remembering what that means. Wisdom will sort out the rest. This way of thinking is the epitome of non-attachment. We are not looking selfishly at what we want, because we know that we are already whole. We are not passively giving ourselves and our wants away, either. Instead, we are looking through the eyes of non-attachment, which I would be so bold as to say through the eyes of love.

I have been asked every time I have taught this what happens if the other person doesn't agree, or gets aggressive? The answer is that you continue being lovingly assertive. If that's not working, be lovingly assertive. **You can never improve on being lovingly assertive.** It's not a set of rules, it is a way of being.

> *"Love is happy when it can give something. The ego is happy when it can take something."*[40]
>
> OSHO

What the Heck Are You Saying?

When we learn to be compassionate rather than sympathetic, we let go of attachment. This allows us to be objective and clear, rather than so immersed in the situation that we cannot function.

By being lovingly assertive, we create a win-win solution for everyone. Watch your life blossom as you use this in every area of your life. It does take practice. And if that practice became your life mission, it would not be in vain.

Practice?

The key to this practice is understanding. Notice where you are when in a conversation or situation. Notice, without judgment, whether you were being aggressive or passive. Just like riding a bike, there will be adjustments to be made, but these adjustments are not intellectual, they are experiential, so trust in the process by taking away the judgment of yourself or others. You will get it wrong, but the more you notice, the closer you will be to naturally being lovingly assertive. This is an implication of wisdom, not an application of mind.

Try starting your day by appreciating who and what is in your life. Journal if you would like, just three pages a day is like a therapy session to me. Try it out, without restriction. You can bitch and moan if you like, then start to see how you can learn from the experience. I feel like I learn something new, or at least deeper, every day.

I have created a morning and evening meditation that helps you fill up your "love tank" as well as looking from lovingly assertive eyes •• use the meditation until you don't have to.

Go to: www.shifthappens.global/freedownloads for the download.

CHAPTER 9

Kick the Shit Out of Triggers: It's an Inside Job

"See that thoughts and feelings are like a train that enters a station and then leaves. Be like the station, not like a passenger."[41]

RUPERT SPIRA

When do feelings of anxiety usually begin?

Sometimes a word or even someone's expression can set us off, but usually we begin our lovely anxiety experience before we get to wherever we are going. It wouldn't be unusual to assume that it's the situation that has created the feelings. But if that were true then everyone on the planet would feel the same way in the same situation. That cannot be and is not the case.

When my wife Andi and I, in the not-so-distant past, were about to go out, especially if it was a networking event or something where we didn't know the people, my wife was, weirdly, excited about meeting new people and socializing. I, on the other hand, was a grumpy old man and a spoiled kid wrapped in one, dreading the extreme pain that these evil new energy vampires were going to inflict on me. I didn't want to spend the whole night with a bunch of judgmental, loud, obnoxious people who wanted to take every ounce of energy that I had, then have the audacity to gossip about how boring I was, even though the reason I was so boring was because they had sucked the life force from my entire body!

Clearly, as you can see, Andi was delusional.

It's common sense to see that you can make up stories about situations, yet you still buy into them, at least feelings-wise. You carry these anxious feelings into a made-up scenario and even keep feeling them after the made-up event, as if you're suffering from PTSD, from an event that didn't even happen, except in your head.

> *"I've lived through some terrible things in my life, some of which actually happened."*[42]
>
> **MARK TWAIN**

Haven't you noticed that people who tend to get angry seem to be constantly having battles with people, places, and things? They seem anxious get themselves in all sorts of anxious situations. A happy-go-lucky type of person just seems to get lucky a lot more often. Things just seem to work out for them.

The most important thing to remember is that our actual default setting is innate well-being; the diamond. We don't have to force good feelings, as we think we do. I did this my whole life, and I'm living proof that it's not a fruitful way to be happy.

What we need to "do" is not do anything in terms of being happy. Just become aware, without judgment. Welcome and accept those limiting thoughts, beliefs, feelings, as if we were welcoming an old friend. Then the feelings will blend into the center of our energy, like a puddle simply blends into a body of water when they touch.

Without resistance, the negative feelings cannot exist, so eventually we will begin to go back to our default setting of positive feelings.

So why TF isn't everyone doing this if it's so damn simple?

Because it's simple, but not easy. You're going against everything that you have learned about protecting yourself. This is virtually impossible during an anxiety attack because you are so fixated on the problem and there is thinking on top of thinking about thinking. Our beliefs are way too strong to be let go of in that moment, without practice and faith that this is how it works. So, it's vital to practice when you are not in a heightened state. Practice on everything and anything so that you get the feel of it. That doesn't sound very motivating, but this is a prevention and a cure. You will find that with practice, you will be able to do this at will, then you won't need to overcome anxiety because it will be a thing of the past.

I often read about the "pressures" of the athletes at the top of their field in the Olympics. It reminded me of when I worked with very elite young tennis players. They were on fire when they were playing a person who was seeded (ranked) higher than them because they were not expected to win. No pressure meant they could just play with nothing to lose, and as a consequence, they often won. Yet when they were seeded higher, they would beat themselves up before, during, and after a game. They put so much pressure on themselves with the fear of losing to a lesser ranked player, unwittingly, as did everyone else, saying to them that this game should be a breeze.

Potential - interference = performance.

If you want to rid yourself of being at the mercy of your circumstances or of any anxiety, then realize that it is only as powerful as the power that you give it. Hear that again please: YOU have the power, not what happens to you.

We are designed to create and to feel good, yet we are taught to deconstruct and become pessimistic. When you feel good more of the time, you will have more of your dreams manifest into reality. Though ironically, you won't care as much as you think, because you will feel good anyway.

Isn't that more powerful than trying to get people to like you, or looking for support, or learning tactics to be great in a crowd? Or figuring out how broken you are and having a ten-year plan (map) on how to fix yourself? Or having plastic surgery? Or taking drugs to stop the feelings of anxiety so that you can at least have an almost ordinary life, not feeling anything? In other words, painting over the illusory shit?

Life is good, buy the T-shirt. I did.

You don't have to think that. You don't have to be that. You are not your anxiety, your shyness, your insecurities, or your ADD. You are a diamond, and when you let go of the illusionary shit and stop wasting energy on building more paint to cover it, your diamond will shine, and your life will begin. Beyond your wildest dreams.

I know I'm repeating myself, but it really is that simple. There's nothing else more valuable that you can learn, to completely—yeah, I said it! —completely change your life for the better, forever!

Most books on social anxiety focus focus on strategies and tactics. But that is like, in the words of Tony Robbins, "Trying to put out a forest fire with a watering can." What we are looking at here is the key to a successful life. In any area of your life, eliminating anxiety is the icing on the cake.

When my wife and I worked with people with addictions and mental disorders in a treatment center, what we found repeatedly was that you could fairly easily treat the symptom, but that did not cure the cause. If one addiction or mental disorder went away, without the root cause being eliminated, another addiction or disorder would take its place. You would be metaphorically excavating some shit off your diamond, but the universe abhors a vacuum, so more shit would eventually replace it.

In every walk of life, you will find someone who has given up alcohol only to be addicted to porn. Or a person treated for anxiety becoming depressed. Because they are not being treated for the cause.

What is the cause?

Is it a chemical imbalance?

Not really, because that's mostly a symptom and not a cause.

Is it low self-esteem? Is it a values issue? Is it from childhood, or any trauma? Is it a significant emotional event?

Yes! All these causes can be put into one word—SHIT!!!! The illusionary shit that covers your diamond.

Realizing this—not just intellectually but experientially—is what will set you free.

None of that shit matters! It seems so important because our societal upbringing has taught us that it is. But it just doesn't matter.

Once you realize that you can be free and let your diamond shine:

You can be creative; you can bring out your creative genius.

You can be sociable, or not, and be okay, regardless of circumstances.

You can sleep at night; you can be comfortable in your own skin.

You can walk and talk and be with natural, not fake, self-esteem.

You can be successful and enjoy the journey.

You can care for others without losing yourself.

You can be kind to others because you don't lack anything and so you have nothing to lose.

You can love unconditionally because you are no longer afraid of losing someone or something. Your cup runneth over with love and happiness.

You can have presence because you will naturally be present.

This is what is on offer when we do the opposite of what we're innocently taught to do.

This seems weird to an introvert perhaps, as you seem to be looking inside all the time. But unfortunately, you're often, if not always, looking inside for critical, judgmental reasons, not the loving ones. We go there to hide, yet we belittle and judge ourselves for doing so. You go within, but only to the level of shit. What I'm talking about is going within for that feeling of fulfillment and joy, of love, peace, and happiness, beyond the shit, to the diamond, your true self. Because that is where all those feelings are. They are not in the social situations that go great, although it feels like it. They're not in the great job, car, social scene, cool friend, hot guy or girl, etc. They are within, and when we can tap into these feelings and emotions, regardless of circumstances, we truly are the masters of our destiny.

We think and feel that it's hard to feel good and not feel anxious, but that's all it is, a way of thinking. A belief even, remember that a belief is a thought that you keep thinking. Thinking that we are at the mercy of our thinking, is what keeps us stuck.

So, the answer is not to think?

No, that's impossible, unless you're a Taoist monk who has dedicated your life to meditation. Even then, the monk doesn't stop thinking all the time, he just stops giving attention to the thoughts. You experience life through thinking. But you have the choice of which thoughts to focus on.

As the quote from Rupert Spira says at the beginning of this chapter, "Be like the station, not a passenger."

Notice he's not suggesting that you close the station down, or police the station to only let certain trains enter. We cannot prevent every thought from coming into our mind (station), but we can decide which thoughts get our attention.

We have been led to believe that we are at the mercy of our circumstances, our thoughts, and our beliefs, but that is a belief in itself. You can either be at the mercy of our thoughts, and they will continue no matter how much positive thinking you do, or you can realize that thoughts will come and go, like the news ticker at the bottom of the TV screen when watching the news. Some will be worthy of your attention. Some will want to be left alone.

Pretending it doesn't exist is not the answer, as this can give the thought power, making it seem like it is in control. Accept it, not as a fact, not as a thing, but as a thought.

The more we can see the "trains of thought" rather than the content of those thoughts, we can stay in control and direct our thinking to the direction we want to go. You don't have to be a monk and dedicate your life to decades of meditation. You can simply realize the truth. Thoughts are not reality, but we see our reality through thought.

I may have frazzled your brain right now with this concept's simplicity.

How about this? We see through our thinking, not through our eyes.

Didn't help?

Our eyes are more like projectors than camera lenses.

We are projecting our thoughts out into the world, combined with our shitty beliefs, which then mingle with the picture that we see, which then comes back to us and is filtered again by our beliefs, values, judgments, etc. By our shit.

Finally, we are conscious of a thought about what we are focused on, heavily filtered by our shitty beliefs. If thought were a food, it would be classed as highly processed and have labels on it.

You can make a massive life change through this new understanding.

You are living in a self-simulated world. Therefore, you believe that your thoughts control you and are out of control. Is it any wonder you can become anxious for no rational reason at any time, in any place?

One person can see a beautiful rose and feel love and happiness. Someone else can see a rose and be afraid because of the thorns and they may have an allergy to roses, in fact, the rose brings back memories of a troubling time which always get triggered when they see a rose. Who's right?

Both! And neither.

Because this is their reality.

A rose is a rose. Whether it's beautiful or terrible is a judgment. In fact, the word rose is a judgment, but hey we must accept some observations just to make sense of things.

The closer we go to just the facts, the more we can go back to our innate well-being.

What are the facts?

The fact is, it's not a rose that we are seeing, we are seeing a mass of past thoughts of what we call a rose.

The world we see is a mirror image of our thoughts.

What Did You Just Say to Me?

- Always remember that our natural default setting is innate well-being, so we don't have to work at it. We do, however, need to practice focusing inside rather than outside.

- The more we become familiar with internal feelings, the less external triggers have any bearing on us.

- We don't see the world; we see a filtered projection of the world. The more we stick to just the facts, the less we get lost in the illusion.

- Accept and welcome feelings but do not buy into thoughts that are heavily processed.

- Potential - Interference = Performance. Our eyes are like projectors; cleaning the interference will help you see clearly and create a life that you love.

Let's Do This!

The most powerful life changing "exercise," although it's more of a reminder, is to let go of judgments. Put a reminder in your phone, catch yourself, and compliment yourself when you do catch yourself. I've mentioned this many times and I cannot mention it enough. It will transform your life for the better, beyond belief.

A great exercise that I learned from the book *The Greatest Secret* by Rhonda Byrne[43] was to welcome an emotion or feeling without judgment or preference, just become aware of it. This lessens any triggers because the feeling is just a feeling until we attach meaning to it.

Now, step into that awareness. This is like the intention of being present, so rather than focusing on the feeling and why you feel it, creating stories and activating triggers, you are bypassing this by focusing on the fact that you are aware of this feeling, and your attention is on the awareness. Now stay in awareness. In fact, you could simply stay in awareness for the rest of your life. That would be the most amazing life that you could ever imagine.

Pattern Interrupts

Two pattern interrupts that I highly recommend:

The first is ho'oponopono, which I first learned from a book called *Zero Limits* by Joe Vitale.[44] I highly recommend that you get the book. I personally like the audiobook and it is read by the author. This is just a ridiculously brief description here.

Ho'oponopono is a Hawaiian prayer of forgiveness in a way, but really its objective is to clean and clear all blockages, traumas, and bad memories and get back to a clean state, to a feeling of lightness, like a weight has been lifted from your shoulders.

This consists of four simple, but very effective, phrases:

1. I'm sorry

2. Please forgive me

3. Thank you

4. I love you

The assumption, in my opinion, is that we are talking to a higher power rather than our ego. We are communicating with our inner being, or the universe, or God. It's whatever you believe is right.

The purpose of this exercise is to connect with the higher powers of forgiveness, gratitude, and love. My understanding is that we are taking responsibility (not blame) for everything in our lives. But the remedy is simply acknowledging this, realizing it is in our thinking, to free up this stuck energy that could be used much more efficiently.

Whenever you feel off track, anxious, or hurt, say these phrases over and over in your head, or out loud if no one is around. Let this mantra clear your thoughts and get back to neutral. We have a reminder in our car, which is especially helpful for me as I encounter some interesting thoughts about the drivers on the road.

These phrases do so much more than I'm giving them credit for here, but for the purposes of this book we will think of them as pattern interrupts to get you out of a stuck state of thinking like anxiety or overwhelm.

You might not want to use all the phrases all the time, or you might choose to say them in a different order. I use different phrases depending on the situation. If I'm feeling good or in a calm situation like doing yoga or meditating, I might just use "thank you" or "I love you." If I'm in more of a negative feeling, I tend to use all four phrases, though not necessarily in the same order. I will repeat the words over and over until I can feel a little calmer and clearer. It's a phenomenal tool to have and, as with most things, it is best to start practicing now. Don't wait until disaster strikes before you start to implement this into your life.

Another book I recommend is *The Tapping Solution* by Nick Ortner. Please go to the website www.thetappingsolution.com[45] because there is a wealth of knowledge there that can show you how to do this and explain the science behind why this works, which is why I purposely am not going to show you in this book. They will most definitely do a better job.

I think of EFT, which stands for "emotional freedom technique," like a self-acupuncture or acupressure technique, because you are tapping on the meridian points of the body which could restore the energy balance that gets thrown off by stress and anxiety.

I'm not an expert on this, so will only point you in the right direction to learn from those that know. My way of doing this is to focus on what I want to feel. So, if I'm feeling anxious, I will want to feel calm. If I'm upset, I may focus on being okay with the situation while tapping on the meridian points to let go of the tension in the body. I also say the ho'oponopono phrases while tapping at the same time and find this super powerful.

Try it out for yourself. Remember, it's not that you are not getting rid of the illusionary shit, because it doesn't exist, except in your mind. You are clearing the waste products that accumulate, as a consequence, in the body.

*"The path to freedom is
not to take life so seriously"*[46]

ANDREA VALLELY

Have you ever noticed how, when someone makes you laugh, you can't help but like them? A little more than you did before, anyway. Have you ever noticed how much better life feels when you're laughing, or just feeling lighthearted? Even your troubles suddenly seem lighter. The person you may have been arguing with doesn't seem so bad.

Learning can be improved. I don't know about you, but the best teachers that seemed to be getting the most out of the kids, including myself, were the teachers who made the subject fun. I remember my geography teacher, who wasn't even funny on purpose, but he was such a character and so passionate and entertaining in how he taught geography that it became one of my favorite subjects.

The less you take life so seriously, the lighter life becomes. Obvious, right? But do we buy into it? And if we do, do we live it? I am, err . . . nearly there. Though, I cannot say I've completely mastered it . . . yet. I do great dad jokes, though.

I love, and want to live by, the phrase that life is too important to be taken seriously. We have been taught to take things seriously, which to a point makes sense, because it means focusing on a subject, but this can be taken way too literally. Being focused is not enhanced by being serious. Think about a movie that was really serious, like one of those dark French movies that, in my mind, never seem to go anywhere. Unless it was very poignant to you, as in the subject was extremely interesting, you probably won't remember much of the film. Then think of a laugh out loud comedy. You will probably be quoting that film for months after seeing that film. I just became a fan of *Seinfeld*, twenty-something years too late, but it wasn't as popular in England, so I never paid much attention before. Now everything is a *Seinfeld* quote.

Okay that's not going to completely convince you to never take anything seriously, so imagine being told to do a test, and this test you must take seriously because it will go towards your final grade. How does that feel? Now imagine your favorite sport that you play or a video game. I bet you got to be good at that game quickly.

Even if you didn't manage to master it, or go professional, I bet you put a lot of "work" into improving yourself in whatever game it was.

The idea that you need to be serious does not guarantee any improvement over actually having a lighthearted enjoyable feeling, given the same importance. And you must admit that feeling lighthearted is a much nicer feeling. It is our innate feeling and helps us to tap into genius. We tap into the zone and this is where the magic happens, where all our filing cabinets of the mind are open to us.

I might get asked "you're telling me that I should be lighthearted at a funeral?" and obviously there are times when we may be sad, and where courtesy would not call for you to be making jokes. But what I'm referring to is an underlying well-being, a feeling of a lighthearted approach to life. This can allow us to not be suckered into believing the shit of limiting beliefs and negative emotions. You become more in touch with your true self, your diamond. Your thoughts become lighter and more positive.

In the words of Sydney Banks, "Life is a contact sport." There are going to be good and bad times, but with this lighthearted view, you will find the good times feel even better and bad times feel easier to handle.

I detest the American habit of greeting each other. Someone says, "Hi, how are you?" And most people reply with a "good, how are you?" I tend to reply with "Fantastico!" Which helps me feel good, though most people don't even notice and go on with their spiel.

Chris Dorris, who does a phenomenal daily dose email (you can subscribe at www.christopherdorris.com)[47] said that when someone asks him how he's doing, he says "This is the best God damn day of my life." I love that, and the obvious question would be to ask why? He says because he chose it to be. (As of writing this, I'm just waiting for an opportunity to say this to someone, though I'll leave out the God damn bit.)

I was once on a Zoom webinar with Michael Neill, who introduced me to the analogy of the diamond that I've used in this book. He was talking with a guy who said that he hated his job. Michael asked, (I'm paraphrasing) "Why would you think that?"

The guy started telling him all the reasons why the job was so terrible. Michael stopped him, saying, "Sorry, but I didn't mean tell me why your job sucks; I meant why would you think that you hate your job?"

That smacked me upside the head! We get so blinded by our perceptions. Yes, you could (and he did) argue that you don't want to hate your job, you just do, because . . . blah blah and don't forget blah. But there's no one forcing you to think that. There's no one forcing you to worry about something or dislike someone or something. You can choose to see it in a different and perhaps more lighthearted way.

It's so deceiving when we get caught up in the circumstances. We say things like, "Well, I didn't hate the previous job so it must be the circumstances." Circumstances can obviously encourage a perception, perhaps a knee-jerk reaction that slips us into a way of thinking, though these are usually just triggers (shit) that we have held on to. But, as Michael Neill so eloquently pointed out, we don't have to think that. Once we realize that we are experiencing stinking thinking about something, even if we think it's justified, we don't have to think that.

I immediately made a list of all the things that I was thinking about that weren't serving me. I vowed then and there not to stop until I had uncovered every thought and change it. Then I got bored and carried on with my life, knowing that I can think whatever the heck I want.

I used to think that I was boring, uninteresting, and not fun to be with. Consequently, I was boring, uninteresting, and not fun to be with. If we imagine that we have a serious problem, we must struggle to fix it, whether mentally or physically, usually both.

This doesn't mean that you must shut up and put up with situations (although it's not uncommon, once your perception changes, to find yourself not even disliking the situation anymore). The person or circumstance could change almost before your eyes. But, if that person or situation is still not good, you will find yourself veering toward something or someone that is more in line with your perception. Rather than being motivated by the negativity of a situation, like the person feeling like they hated their job, you will find that you're inspired to move in a new direction; moving towards what you want rather than away from what you don't want.

It's like magic, naturally.

So, am I saying your whole life can change for the better simply by changing your perception? Yes!

Okay, let me put it another way. Oh, hell yeah!

The only thing preventing you from having a wonderful life free of social, or any form of anxiety and lack, is the belief that you need to change anything but your perception. Imagine if you made this your life's work? If you dedicated yourself to realizing and changing perceptions to what you want to see in life, you will have the most amazing life experience. That's what I've done, and I want that for you, too. I'm not talking about painting on a perception, I'm talking about a true change in the direction of your thinking. Coming from the diamond.

Don't Ask How, Ask Who

The only thing preventing you from having a great and enjoyable social life is your perceptions about your social life. Trust me, I'm sure you are probably coming up with thousands of reasons why you disagree with me. And that's because of your perception about it. (I can be a real dick at times.)

I wanted to believe this for decades, but it felt almost impossible when so much evidence was to the contrary. My shit seemed so real. I perceived that shit to be the truth. I would "try" to put the new perception into practice. I would go out, throw myself in the deep end, be drowned by an awkward situation, and then decide that there must be more to it than that.

But perception is a super-strong illusion, and it's all you know. If you perceive that social, or any anxiety, is out of your control, but trying to think the opposite, you are setting yourself up for failure. You're trying to defy your thermostat. Ain't gonna happen.

So how?

Compound Interest!

First, remember that we live in the feeling of our thinking, moment to moment, not what's happening outside of us. This is the missing link: from intellectually doing to being. Don't think . . . FEEL. Don't focus on your thoughts and try to change them; you will fail because it's pretty much an impossibility. But with the perception of, let's say enjoying social interactions, you can notice the feeling of that.

If that's too much, which admittedly it was for me, you can simply get into a good feeling state without labeling the feeling itself. When you veer off to a low feeling like uncertainty or anxiety, which you will, you can simply notice it, take a breath, allow the feelings, and allow yourself to let go. Then be immersed in your surroundings, not forcing any feelings, just being.

Be patient. Your shit habit is strong. Keep doing this, remembering the truth that you're the diamond and focusing on how you want to feel. When you get an emotion, feeling, or circumstance that is positive, you can milk that for all it's worth for as long as it's giving you good energy. As soon as you feel like it's becoming work, then it's done.

You can (though I wouldn't recommend this at first) go into detail and look at specifics when the feeling is good, but be wary and stick only to the facts when the feeling is not so good—simple. A good rule of thumb is describing a negative situation or feeling with one sentence maximum and only once, whereas a positive describe in five sentences and as often as you like.

It's vitally important to practice this in incremental, achievable steps. Don't go throwing yourself into the deep end. Start with something small. Go to a cafe and order a drink with your perception of feeling comfortable. Look inward and notice your feelings; don't worry about people's reactions.

If you find yourself falling back, allow, accept, let go, and continue. Leave if it's too uncomfortable, then go back another day. This is better than fighting it and hoping that you can break through. Go slow. If it still feels bad, notice without judgment, and adjust to what feels comfortably uncomfortable. Keep doing this until it's natural and feels comfortable. Then move on to something else. But, and I cannot emphasize this enough, not until you are comfortably uncomfortable with that situation. Please don't rush this, take your time. Before you know it, you will be comfortable pretty much everywhere you go. And you will find yourself wanting to go to more places, maybe even pushing the boundaries once you have built up to that stage. This works like compound interest: it looks like nothing is changing at first, but as you stick with it, it starts to build so rapidly that it seems like a miracle has happened . . . because it has.

Be patient. This will change your life, so don't rush it. Be kind to yourself as you're doing this.

Keep focusing on your feelings, not people's reactions, constantly letting go of judgments. It's very addicting to get suckered back into looking outside ourselves for reassurance. The more you can notice your feelings without judging them, the more you will find other people's reactions change for the better, because you are feeling better, and it acts like a mirror effect. People feel comfortable and safe around people who are comfortable in themselves.

What's great is that it doesn't matter anyway. If you are feeling good, it's all good.

It's just like the unwritten rule of giving: when you give in order to receive, you get nothing back, because it was a fake giving and it has a price tag. When you give with no agenda, with no expectation of receiving anything, you will receive a hundredfold, maybe a thousandfold.

When you are trying to feel comfortable so that people will like you, they will feel the underlying feeling and not feel comfortable because they feel this incongruence in you. When you are naturally comfortable, people will love being around you without you doing a thing, because your energy speaks volumes.

We create our lives through thought and feeling, we then live in that creation via our perception and in our feelings. We cannot change the thought, but we can change our perception and our feelings, creating new thinking. When we live without constant judgments, we stay in our present moment experience. Then "fear" (anxiety and worry) cannot continue.

I remember my first (of many) fire walk experiences.[48] If you don't know what this is, it's a bunch of crazy people that make a bed of coals roughly a mile long, with the average temperature of 1,000,000 degrees Fahrenheit or so. Then, even crazier dudes like me pay them to let us walk over those molten coals, chanting a mantra in our heads. The idea, of course, is to show what's possible when we get out of our own way. My first experience didn't go so well. I got burned.

I did my prep and managed to not look at the crowd that was either side of this 200-mile-or-so stretch of burning magma (it gets longer every time I tell this story). Ridiculously, I was more anxious about the crowd watching me than the fire.

It started well. I was chanting away in my head "Cool moss, cool moss," it's a long story but that was the chant. Halfway through I was really going strong, not rushing, not feeling anything. You could say I was in the zone, until, in the corner of my eye, I saw a young kid, just looking at me from under the rope that was separating the people from the idiots like me who are walking on the surface of the sun.

I must've thought that he might walk onto the coals and hurt himself, but he was fine, just short. This was all in a split second, but it broke my concentration. I suddenly became aware of everyone staring at me, then . . . I felt the burning of my toes. The next half of my walk was like something out of a comedy sketch, as I almost ran through the rest of the "walk" and my mantra went from "cool moss" to "ohh, ow, oooo, ow, ohh, oh, ow!!"

I've partaken in dozens of fire walks since, even though that first experience should've put me off of them for life. But it was a perfect example of how, when we get into our heads, we burn, metaphorically and sometimes physically, yet when we are in the zone, it's like we float through life, enjoying the feeling. Or not feeling at all. I don't mean being numb to feelings, just having a natural calm.

This is why the technique of focusing on the other person when socializing can be flawed, which I experienced myself. If you try to focus on the other person to take the pressure off yourself, you are consciously thinking about the person, yet unconsciously feeling vulnerable and not comfortable in yourself. This creates that incongruence. As discussed before, it is better than nothing; however, you cannot help but feel vulnerable, and eventually you will revert to being self-conscious of your illusionary shit.

What if you realized that you really are the diamond? That there's nothing to be self-conscious about?

Think about this.

Awareness is not aware of awareness, that's just looking at a version of awareness. I know that's a little confusing, but there's a point here. I love what Rupert Spira once said in a talk. He said to stand up and take a step toward yourself.

Impossible, right? So how can you be aware of awareness? You can be aware of being aware, but you cannot look at yourself being aware. You are awareness. That is your true self. The diamond. The diamond is not aware of itself; it just is.

You are not aware of yourself when you are in the zone, you just are. So, as a description of what happens, rather than a prescription of what to do, when you are in the zone you are *naturally* only ever aware of the person in front of you. Because awareness is never aware of itself, it's completely comfortable.

You never need to force this when you are truly comfortable in your skin. That, my friend, is incredibly life-changing, and much rarer than you (and most people who think that they're comfortable in their skin) realize.

Okay What?

- Lighten up, it literally lightens your life.

- Talk about how you want to feel in detail and as often as you like. Let go of any heavy feelings in one sentence and speak it only once.

- Don't try to change your thoughts. Change your perception and go by your feelings.

- Life without judgment will give you everything you ever wanted. It's possibly the fastest way to freedom from anxiety.

- You are the diamond, there's no need to try to be anything, just allow yourself to be.

- You never need to be, and cannot be, aware of awareness; just be in awareness. This is the key to being truly comfortable in your own skin.

Create Compound Interest

When I used to teach people how to activate their core muscles in the midsection, most wanted to rush to the hard exercises without being able to hold the activation, which not only defeats the object, but could also cause injury. They would start by lying down, then go to a seated position, then to standing, etc., and not move to the next level until they could activate the core in the previous position. This is what we want to accomplish here. The feeling of being comfortably uncomfortable is like the activation of the core; if you lose that at any time then you know you have gone too far.

Ask yourself what you want. Maybe socially or otherwise.

Now think of a time when you felt comfortable in your own skin. If you cannot think of a time, then imagine how it feels. The feelings are within us, even if they've been buried deep inside.

Now take the next step toward that intent. So, let's say you want to feel comfortable socially, or even really enjoy social events. What could be the first step that you can take in that direction? You might think of going to a library or coffee shop, for instance. We're using compound interest, so go slow. Depending on your comfort level and whether you can keep this feeling of well-being will determine how far you go, and it is advisable to go slower than you think you can.

The first step might be to walk into a library, look at some books on the shelf, and walk out, all the time noticing how you are feeling without judgment and looking for that comfortable feeling. If you lose the feeling, then walk out and adjust accordingly. You may go again tomorrow, or you may find that it was too much for the first time, so only walk to the entrance of the building. Trust me, the purpose of this is to feel the feelings, so it's not important to push yourself too much.

Please let me know how this goes for you. If you have any questions send me an email at lee.vallely@yahoo.com.

*"Nothing outside of you can harm or help you.
It's all in the feelings. A picture is worth
a thousand words, but a feeling
is worth a thousand pictures."*

LEE VALLELY

Imagine what it costs to have so many preferences. Imagine having no preferences? What would your life be like? I'm guessing you probably think that life would be chaos, that people would walk all over you, and you would never achieve anything or do anything because hey, what's the point? But, as I've mentioned a lot I know, to get the point fixed firmly in your mind, your innate well-being is positive. The only thing getting in your way of having a blissful, fulfilling life is your preferences, aka judgments, aka your shit.

So, am I suggesting that you give up every preference you have? Yes. Only because you won't be able to. It pushes us in the right direction to break free of the illusion that we have created, which makes it almost impossible to win, or at least enjoy, the game of life. We have so many preferences that we tie ourselves in knots.

You must let go of everything you think you are to be who you are.

We will fight to protect our ego, both literally and figuratively. If someone insults your car, does that mean you are scarred for life? If you say yes, then please seek medical attention immediately. Although I have had (many) times in my life that it would be true for me, too.

I was so sensitive to criticism in the past that it felt like I took *everything* personally. So, please make sure that once you've read this book that you write a nice review. I'm sensitive.

We know logically that just because someone doesn't have the same taste, the same preference, in other words, in cars, partners, politics, or dress sense, it doesn't mean that you are physically or mentally damaged by this.

Unless, of course, you are so connected to things that you cannot distinguish where you end and the outside world begins.

Here is where the attachment is and why preferences create your problems. If you have no preferences, how can you have a problem? In my mind, the problem is distinguishing between what you want compared to what you have—be that a person, place, or thing. So, if someone has "insulted" you, they have said or done something that is not how you want it to be, whether that's how you want to be thought of, or something that is perhaps not true.

I am not saying that you must not defend yourself or acknowledge wrongs in any way, but when we are not so attached to how others perceive us, we don't find the need to defend so much. We realize that other people's opinions, judgments, and preferences have no bearing on our identity.

I love the saying that whatever people think of you is none of your business. That's a very freeing idea to adopt, and by adopting this understanding, you will find that your life has so much more clarity than ever before.

We have established that anxiety tends to be irrational; otherwise, it would simply be pure fear, which is a good thing for self-preservation. If you are crossing the road and suddenly see a bus coming toward you, or just sense it, you will be glad that you have a safety mechanism called fear (our fight-or-flight response) that puts your body into a superhuman-like state of alertness, and you find yourself diving out of the way of the oncoming bus.

That wasn't a preference. You didn't start rationalizing in your head whether you wanted to be crushed by a bus or whether you would rather not be. You just jumped in the air and got out of the way. That's built into us; we don't need to be as defensive and on alert to attack as we think, we can trust our natural awareness to keep us safe. The rest is almost certainly our ego taking offense.

But anxiety is taking all sorts of scenarios and making internal judgments leading to that fight-or-flight response to be tricked into being constantly switched on. So, without realizing it, going to a place or event can be interpreted by your brain to be as bad as being run over by a bus.

Let me ask you something: are you prejudiced? If you said no, I call bullshit, because everyone on this planet is prejudiced in some way. You might think that you are a "live and let live, everyone can be themselves" kind of person. Bullshit.

I'm not saying that you are evil for being prejudiced; it's just a misunderstanding of how and why you are. Our mind makes connections to outside stimulus. Just like a computer can notice patterns and come to a mathematical conclusion, our mind makes these connections and draws conclusions based on information received.

Notice that I didn't say we, I said our mind, saying that we are our mind is like saying that we are our car.

I was in a leadership seminar once where the speaker asked us to close our eyes and answer to ourselves, are we prejudiced? I thought about it and couldn't truthfully say that I wasn't. He then asked us, with our eyes closed, to put our hands up if we were. I did. Then he asked us to stand up if we were. I did, but was a little apprehensive at this point, wishing I hadn't committed by putting my hand up. Then the mother-loving soul asked us to open our eyes and look around the room. Half of the people were also standing up. All of them should have been, really, but it was a great example of us thinking that we were the only ones when we all, okay most (that will admit it), feel this way.

So going back to the New York example from an earlier chapter. I will have a prejudiced view of New York based on my experience. If I were forced to go there again, I would go there looking for confirmation of my presumption of what New York is like based on my previous experience. So, more than likely I will find more proof to back my claim that New York stinks. Why? Because I will be looking for it, maybe somewhat consciously, but mostly sub-consciously, presuming it as a fact. I may talk to the front desk with perhaps a little sarcasm in my voice, so I get a courteous, though not-so-pleasant, response from them. "See? I knew all New Yorkers are rude!" The list goes on.

Can you see how this relates to social, or any, anxiety?

You go with apprehension to a party or meeting, and without realizing it, you have made assumptions and created a prejudiced situation. Then, the people greet you with apprehension. It seems like people are avoiding you, not realizing that you have your resting bitch face on. This is our life, and we are, most of the time, oblivious to it.

Some prejudices are blatantly obvious, like if someone is a member of the KKK, but most are not. The fewer preferences we hold on to, the fewer prejudices we hold onto, and the more our natural curiosity, assertiveness, and love comes through.

We find ourselves. Not our egotistical self, but our true self.

Potential – Interference = Performance

I used to use an example in my seminars where I would place a dot in the middle of a whiteboard and say that this dot represents the problem, so everything else is not the problem. Yet when we're focused on that dot, it's like everything is the problem, and there is no solution, or not the problem.

We can get out of our limited thinking and making our "problems" so huge and impenetrable, when we realize that everything else is not the problem; there are infinite ways to improve the situation. Unfortunately, we put our preferences as the dot and everything else is not our preference, making it almost impossible to feel better. Take away the dot altogether and watch your world expand for the better before your eyes. The problem tends to only exist because something is opposite to your preference.

Don't get obsessed with the outcome, get passionate about the process.

Pretty much every practice I've encountered in self-help / personal development has some form of letting go, be that the problem or the belief. I have found that for most of my life I've been trying to overcome or strengthen my will. I have been under the illusion that if I were stronger and used more willpower, I would be able to create.

I now realize that it's the opposite. I realized that I "just" need to let go. Not even letting go, because that sounds like a need to "do" something, I simply learned to get out of my own way.

Laughter Is the Best Medicine

Laughter is the best medicine, and this is taken so lightly, pardon the pun. Why do we feel better when we laugh? Why are we drawn to people who make us laugh? Because we "forget" ourselves. What are we forgetting? The pretense of the paint that covers the shit.

Because we are immersed in the story, we lose ourselves, and, without realizing it, we let go of troubles, judgments, and "problems" (please let go of calling them that).

So, we could think that we need to be around comedians and storytellers the whole time, and while that would be fun and a much better idea than being around naysayers or watching the news, it's more advantageous long-term to realize why it works. And it does work.

We tend to look objectively through a subjective mind. One situation can be fearful, or we can be rejected by one person, then we create an objective perception that every situation or person will be the same.

Let that shit go.

Don't Be a Shit Actor

This is a very controversial topic. A lot of people may disagree with my opinion. Apart from Bob Proctor, author of many fabulous books including *The Art of Living,* and known as the narrator of the movie *The Secret.*[49]

Here's my take on it, based loosely on what I was taught by Bob Proctor. The reason I say loosely is because I don't totally agree with full-on acting as if. Let me explain.

There's a huge difference between faking it till you make it and acting as if. Faking it till you make it requires effort and constant vigilance to make sure that you are doing the things that make you "look and sound" like the person or attribute that you are faking. Underneath this fakeness is a knowing that you are just faking; you don't really believe it. There are countless great comedians and actors who seem to have it all, only to find out later that they are suffering. They stopped acting and then went back to believing the shit. An actor is that person only for a role, but you must become that person 24/7 for the rest of your life! Acting as if is becoming that person, or if it's a situation, becoming the person who lives in that situation, immersing in the situation or states of that person, not pretending, learning lines, and tools and strategies to fake it. You think like that person, embodying that persona.

You become that person.

Once you become, you no longer need to think of how that person would react, because you just are. You move like that person, not because you've practiced how they move (although you may have at the beginning, only to get the feeling of being), but because it's you, that's how you move. Most of your personality has come about through learned behavior, so our minds can learn another personality.

Faking it is like adopting some healthy ways of eating and reminding yourself to stick to this way of eating. Acting is being a healthy person eating naturally the way healthy people eat.

We don't feel anxiety because of the situation, so faking it till you make it is looking in the wrong place, trying strategies to fix an illusionary situation, but then falling back into the belief of an anxious person. We suffer from anxiety because we're recreating the act of anxiety over and over again. A thought, and therefore a feeling, will disappear if we give no power to it.

You might argue, as would and did I, that you're not even thinking any thoughts of anxiety, they just happen. That's because you're thinking (acting) like an anxious person who must be vigilant of these thoughts that may take over at any moment. If you were a person who didn't suffer from social, or any, anxiety, you would not need to waste your energy on this kind of thinking because you wouldn't have those thoughts, or, more accurately, even if you did, so what? They have no power over you, they would shrink without you even noticing. Like elevator music, they are merely in the background.

Thoughts have no power by themselves. We have the power to create mountains out of molehills, and molehills out of mountains. We can create the perfect relationship, or the relationship from hell, without moving from our chairs. With the same circumstances, through our attention to certain ways of thinking, we create heaven or hell. Our thoughts and our thinking are based on our identity.

Our thoughts have no power behind them; a thought by itself has no meaning until we give it meaning through our perception. Our thinking has the power of our perception behind it. That's a very mighty power, and isn't it ironic (don't ya think?) that it's us who created that very power that has debilitated us all these years.

Awareness is the key here (non-judgmental awareness remember). Now you know what is going on inside your mind. Trying to fix your thinking is going against your thermostat. Yet when we observe without judgment, the habits begin to fall away as they are exposed.

The cat is out of the bag, so now what? Now you go about your life knowing that you are no longer at the mercy of this illusionary anxiety because you have seen that it is an illusion. Like when the magician unveils the trick, you cannot be fooled in the same way again.

If I told you a much better way to get to work, that's much simpler and quicker way than the route you're taking now, and will take twenty minutes less time, you will not need to be told more than once, you will simply go that way from now on. You may fall into the old way a couple more times out of habit or not paying attention, but as soon as you realize that you've gone the old way, you will return to the new way ASAP.

I must warn you, though, it's so easy to read this and just dismiss it without putting the ideas into practice. I'm guilty of that, which is why I urge you to, maybe after a week or so, read this book again, even if it's just the summaries.

Burn this part into your mind. Your thoughts have no power, they are directed by your perception. Change your perception and act as if you are the person that you want to be (truly are in fact) for the rest of your life!

We are so distracted in this world, especially when in the midst of feeling anxiety, that it's almost impossible to focus on anything. Repetition is the mother of skill, so even if you just read the summaries and the final chapter, you'll see something that you didn't feel before.

And please, please, please get in touch with me at lee.vallely@ yahoo.com or through messenger. I know this can work for you, not (just) because I'm so smart, but because it's the Truth, so if you're not getting the results, then I can help you.

A belief is a recurring thought or thoughts. You cannot stop your thoughts, but you can take your attention from one and insert instead a different thought that you want to focus on. So, you may believe (a thought you keep thinking) that you cannot break this anxiety cycle, because that's what it is: it's the fight or flight response that gets triggered over and over.

But if you take your attention from that belief, knowing that it's merely a continuous thought that you've given way too much attention to, and then focus on the truth, that you can focus on the perception that you are safe and comfortable, you eventually transfer that debilitating belief to a belief that serves you. Now it's no longer acting, it's the truth of who you are.

I am angry, I am anxious, I am shy . . . is not true. You may feel these things, created by your perception, but it is not who you are. You can drop these beliefs by letting go of all those labels.

If we could only see that the feelings we feel are created by our thinking, not because of the world, we would be able to let these feelings dissipate. But we are so programmed to be reactive to any "bad" feelings that we think that they are unbearable.

Who are you?

When you say or think "I am . . ." stop before you continue and leave it as I AM.

This pause is the key to tapping into the self and not being suckered into the illusionary shit world that our imagination has manufactured. It's like watching a movie but not really connected to the story because you are aware that it's not real.

I remember watching a series called *This Is Us*[50] with Andi, my wife. Something happened, I can't even remember what it was, but Andi was bawling her eyes out and I, being the loving husband that I am, didn't even notice and asked if she wanted tea. I was completely neutral to the screen, but Andi was connected to the characters as if they were real. It sounds terrible and I promise I am not as unfeeling as it sounds, I just happened to not be immersed in the story.

When we can see the "movie" of our lives without being overly connected, but still having compassion and caring, we will be more loving, more helpful, and so much more selfless with our time and attention, with self-esteem that would be beyond our capabilities if we are deeply connected with our beliefs about a situation. When we're connected too much it can be an obligation rather than coming from a place of loving understanding and compassion because we are taking everything personally.

I have a horrible confession, I'm seriously not proud of this. My Gran was an obligation to me toward the last years of her life. I was always there for her but felt obligated rather than lovingly compassionate. My thoughts and feelings of our past and of my judgments, of my triggers and personal emotions, were connected. If I could have been detached (not indifferent as that's a cold dismissal of a person or situation), if I could have been unattached to the emotions, I would have been so much more compassionate, loving, and caring. I would have been enjoying my experience with her so much more.

Please understand that I wasn't horrible and didn't neglect her, I'm talking about my feelings and emotions internally. Instead of being present and enjoying our time together, I wanted to get it over with. I was internally uncomfortable rather than enjoying being with my Nan.

Externally, nothing would have changed. I wouldn't have done anything differently or been there any more often. The experience would have been much more fruitful, though, because people can feel your energy.

We are all expert bullshit detectors; we can tell when someone doesn't want to be around us. I'm sure my Nan felt my crappy energy and I really regret that.

I don't dwell on it because that doesn't serve anyone. But I do not forget, as it's a painful reminder not to get sucked into that way of thinking ever again in my life. Why let anyone feel that way, especially my own family? I vow never to feel like I don't want to be around anyone again as much as I can help it.

How do you do that?

There's no need to force yourself to like people; that's going against what this whole book is about. When you can stop looking for something or someone to make you feel better, you will be happy and free of the illusionary shackles of anxiety. This will automatically change the way you respond to others. Put attention to the feelings, not the content. This takes judgment of the person away. Feelings can be deceiving; one minute you can feel disgust for a person, yet if they fell and broke their leg in that moment, all bad feelings would disappear and feelings of concern would replace them (hopefully). I've said to focus on feelings, but that doesn't mean that you believe your feelings are truth, they are merely a consequence of your perceptions.

Emotions are transient and fleeting if we let them continue on their way without resistance. We are the ones that hold onto them, mostly unconsciously. So let them go and see your life, and energy, lift.

By changing our mindset step by step, we can create a miraculous life without anxiety. So, what are the steps?

Notice, notice, notice. Without attaching judgment.

> *"Nothing will be attempted, if all possible objections must first be overcome."*[51]
>
> SAMUEL JOHNSON

Noticing without judgment. Letting go of all judgments and resentments of anyone and everyone. Taking a deep breath and accepting these judgments, then exhaling and either saying and feeling, or just feeling, the stuck negative energy dissolves in its own time. This may take a while, but persevere. It may even take more than one go at it. Be patient and kind to yourself, this is a process. It will work if you persevere without judgment, I said without judgment. When you find yourself judging, which you will, notice you are judging, without judgment.

I know, it's annoying (that's a judgment), but it's the most freeing exercise to completely transform your life. So please stick with it, and PLEASE don't overthink or complicate it. It really is this simple. Not easy, but definitely this simple. You will want to do anything else but this at times, because your ego will be fighting you.

Always remember to breathe in and out through the nose. Breathe into your heart and allow yourself to be in a state of calm.

Think of the 3D exercise. Whenever you are feeling anything negative, and especially when there is a story attached to it, 3D it:

> **Delete:** This is deleting the story, the feelings, and any energy attached to the situation.

> **DE story:** This is reinforcing this deletion so that nothing remains, never breathing the story again.

> **DE create:** This is going back to the source of all creation so that not only have you let it go but made it so that it never even existed.

Like everything we have spoken about, don't ANALyze or over-think this, simply say it or think it and trust that it has worked, then focus on the loving happy being that you are 24/7.

"Be calm; yet assertive.
Be meek; yet courageous.
Be gentle; yet bold.
Be kind; yet strong."[52]

CHARLES F GLASSMAN

I know this hasn't exactly been a stereotypical book, yet I think by now you know that the answer is not in the strategies, it's in you already.

If you find it confusing, I'm not surprised. Please read through again, or, at the very least, review the summaries. This is life changing, so I really urge you to go through this like a life changing course. Because it really is life changing. Read a chapter a week, then put into action what you learn from that chapter.

It might take a while for the simplicity to sink in. Sydney Banks said that within the simplicity lies the complexities of life.

You are the diamond, not the shit. You are the sun, not the clouds.

No matter how dark it seems under the clouds, the sun is not darkened.

No matter how much shit you have accumulated, you, the diamond, are intact and shining regardless.

We don't need to fix the weather; we need to understand that it's just how the weather is.

We don't need to fix our so-called faults, we just need to realize that it's just shit created by changes in circumstances and atmospheres, just like the weather.

We can do nothing to change the weather, but we can dress accordingly. The great philosopher who you may not have heard of in the USA, Billy Connolly, (who was also a comedian and actor in his spare time) said that there is no such thing as bad weather, just insufficient clothing.

Put the right clothes on and know that "this too shall pass." Clear the shit by welcoming, as awareness, step into awareness and stay as long as you can in awareness. Use the 3Ds to delete, destory, and decrease any negative feelings or thoughts through all time, space, and matter. Then do heart breathing in and out through the nose, just for the rest of your life.

Without reading the book, these would be just another set of tools, but with the realization of why you are doing these exercises you will make a massive transformation.

People sometimes tend to say, "Then what?" Then you will know what to do, because until that moment comes, no one can tell the future 100 percent. But with this knowledge, you can be assured that the answer will appear when the time is right. It does take a lot of practice, so remember baby steps, incremental changes.

Be kind to yourself. This is not a quick fix, it's a lifestyle transformation.

There are quite a lot of exercises to put into action, but they're not the answer. The answer is to understand where your experience is coming from. You are a diamond, but the shit is who you think you are, so you cover the illusionary shit with paint to resemble a diamond, not knowing that you are already not only as good, but way, way better than any paint you can find.

So why even bother to add exercises if they're not necessary?

The exercises give you an option of interrupting the pattern of thinking to bring you back to the truth. To give temporary, not permanent, relief while knowing that they are not the answer. The truth is what will set you free. They allow you to release the energy trapped inside those feelings. You are metaphorically putting on the clothing relevant to the weather.

So, do you need to do all of them? No, though I suggest that you try them all out to see which ones soothe you better, depending on the weather, aka the circumstance and your preference in the moment.

And if you still are finding it really difficult (not just ordinarily difficult, because it will be), shoot me an email at lee.vallely@ yahoo.com. Or message me on Facebook. Join my Facebook group: kickthesh.toutof. I cannot guarantee an instant response, but I can guarantee a response. I know what it's like to feel like you're doing this alone, but you are not alone.

I want you to break this unnecessary suffering forever. It took me decades to get to this understanding, so if it takes you a few months to really get it, you are still way ahead of the game, because most people never get this.

It's simple, but it takes courage, faith, and practice.

I wish you well, my friend.

I finish this very weird, but super effective book about social anxiety with a quote from the amazing poet Rumi: "Out beyond ideas of wrongdoing and right doing there is a field. I'll meet you there."[52]

With all my love,
Lee, the shit eliminator

Acknowledgments

I have so, so many people to thank that it would be unjust to try to make a list. But there is one person who I absolutely must acknowledge, that is my wife, Andrea Vallely.

She is my soulmate, my rock, and is almost as good a cook as me 😋 Thank you for being on this amazing journey with me Andrea 🤍

Endnotes

1. Shakespeare , William. *A Midsummer Night's Dream (Arden Shakespeare: Second Series). Second.* Arden Shakespeare, 1979.

2. "Facts and Statistics." Anxiety and Depression Association of America, ADAA. Accessed March 15, 2024. https://adaa.org/.

3. Oprah. "Oprah and Amy Schumer on Being Secret Introverts." Oprah.com http://Oprah.com/"*Harris, Dan. 10% happier.* New York, NY: It Books, 2014.

4. Grinder, John, and Richard Bandler. "Definition of NLP." The Association for Neuro Linguistic Programming. Accessed March 5, 2024. https://anlp.org/.

5. Neill, Michael. *The inside-out revolution: The only thing you need to know to chance your life forever.* Carlsbad, CA: Hay House, 2013.

6. "The Wizard of Oz." IMDb, August 25, 1939. https://www.imdb.com/title/tt0032138/.

7. Used with permission. "It's like a Finger Pointing Away to the Moon. Don't Look at the Finger or You Will All That Heavenly Glory." - Bruce Lee." Be Water My Friend" Bruce Lee. Accessed March 4, 2024. https://brucelee.com/. The Bruce Lee Quote is Copyright of Bruce Lee Enterprises, LLC. All Rights Reserved. www.brucelee.com

8. Robbins, Tony. "Tony Robbins - the Official Website of Tony Robbins." tonyrobbins.com, February 1, 2024. https://www.tonyrobbins.com/.

9. *Spira, Rupert. The nature of consciousness: Essays on the unity of mind and matter. Oxford: Sahaja Publications, 2017. And the analogy of John Smith.*

10. "Brain Facts 70000 Thoughts per Day." Healthy Brains by Cleveland Clinic,

May 11, 2020. https://healthybrains.org/brain-facts/.

11. Pransky, George. "The Relationship Handbook." Pransky & Associates, 1991. https://www.pranskyandassociates.com

12. Twain, Mark. "Top 10 Mark Twain Quotes - Brainyquote." If we learned, 2024. https://www.brainyquote.com/lists/authors/top-10-mark-twain-quotes.

13. Cameron, Julia. *Artist's way: 25th anniversary edition.* Penguin Books, 2016.

14. Gallwey, W. Timothy. *The inner game of tennis.* New York, New York : Random House, 1974.

15. Smart, Jamie. *Results: Get clarity, achieve results.* Chichester, West Sussex: Capstone, 2016.

16. Banks, Sydney. *The enlightened gardener.* Lone Pine Publishing, 2016.

17. Hawkins, David R. *Power vs. force: The hidden determinants of human behavior.* Carlsbad, CA, Ca: Hay House, Inc., 2014.

18. "King of Queens." Episode. *King of Queens* All, no. All. Tbs.com, 1998.

19. Nelligan, TJ, and Theresa Foy DiGeronimo. *Live like Sean: Important life lessons from my special-needs son.* Austin, TX: Greenleaf Book Group Press, 2021.

20. Braden, Gregg. *Wisdom codes: Ancient words to rewire our brains and heal our hearts.* Australia: Hay House Inc, 2020.

21. Baugh, Nathan. "NASA Researchers Found 98% of 5 Year Olds Are Creative Geniuses." LinkedIn, 2023. https://www.linkedin.com/.

22. McCourt, Lisa. *Free your joy: The twelve keys to sustainable happiness.* Deerfield Beach: Health Communications, 2023.

23. Darwin, Charles. ""It Is Not the Strongest of the Species That Survives, Not the Most Intelligent That Survives. It Is the One That Is the Most Adaptable to Change." Goodreads, 2024. https://www.goodreads.com/.

24. Wachowski, Lilly, Lilly Wachowski, Lana Wachowski, Lana Wachowski, Joel Silver, Don Davis, Bill Pope, Owen Paterson, Zach Staenberg, and Yuen Wo Ping. *The matrix,* n.d.

25. "Captain Cook." Essay. In *What the Bleep Do We Know.* 20th century fox, n.d.

26. Dwoskin, Hale. *The Sedona Method: How to get rid of your emotional baggage and live the life you want*. London: Element, 2005.

27. Cooley, Charles Horton. "'I Am Not What I Think I Am, and I Am Not What You Think I Am. I Am What I Think You Think I Am.' ⊠ Charles Horton Cooley." Goodreads. Accessed March 5, 2024. https://www.goodreads.com/.

28. "Page 76 Story of Muscle Memory Gone Wrong." Essay. In *On Combat: The Psychology and Physiology of Deadly Conflict in War and in Peace*, 2007.

29. Maxwell, John. "Making an Impression vs Being Impressed." Maxwell Leadership |, June 2011. https://www.johnmaxwell.com/.

30. With permission. Mooji. "'If You Could Truly Look inside the Heart of Any and Every Single Human Being, You Would Fall in Love with Them Completely." Quote by Mooji is (c) Mooji Media Ltd 2024, www.mooji.org

31. Debenham, Anna, Susan Marmot, and Paul Lock. "Beyond Recovery Is the UK's Leading 3P Social Enterprise Working within the Criminal Justice System." Beyond Recovery, May 24, 2023. https://beyond-recovery.co.uk/.

32. Ziglar, Zig, and Nor Junainah Masjuni. *See you at the top*. Batu Caves, Selangor: PTS Publications, 2015.

33. With permission from Patent, Arnold M. *You can have it all*. Pymble, N.S.W.: HarperCollins, 1996.

34. Bandler, Richard. *Get the life you want*. Deerfield Beech, FL: Health Communications Inc., 2023. Bandler, Richard. "Legacy of the Master." Goodreads, 2024. https://www.goodreads.com/book/show/203329076-legacy-of-the-master.

35. Osho. *The book of understanding*. Crown Publishing Group, 2006.

36. Eiseley, Loren. "Starfish Story." Goodreads. Accessed March 4, 2024. https://www.goodreads.com/.

37. *Pay it forward* . Burbank, CA.: Warner Home Video, 2001.

38. Ross, Don. "Game Theory." Stanford Encyclopedia of Philosophy, 2023. https://plato.stanford.edu/.

39. Osho. "Love Is Happy When It Is Able to Give Something. The Ego Is Happy When It Is Able to Take Something. ." The Hans India. Accessed March 4, 2024. https://www.thehansindia.com/.

40. Twain, Mark. "I've Lived through Some Terrible Things in My Life, Some of Which Actually Happened." Goodreads. Accessed March 4, 2024. https://www.goodreads.com/.

41. Byrne, Rhonda, and Francesca Pe'. *The greatest secret*. Milano: HarperCollins, 2021.

42. Vitale, Joe, and Haleakalā Hew Len. *Zero limits: The secret Hawaiian system for wealth, health, peace, and more*. Hoboken, NJ: Wiley, 2009.

43. Ortner, Nick. *The tapping solution: A revolutionary system for stress-free living*. Carlsbad, Cal.: Hay House, 2014.

44. Dorris, Chris. "The Mental Toughness Coach, Chris Dorris." The Mental Toughness Coach - Chris Dorris. Accessed March 4, 2024. http://www.christopherdorris.com/.

45. Robbins, Tony. "Tony Robbins Firewalk." Tony Robbins. Accessed March 4, 2024. https://tonyrobbinsfirewalk.com/.

46. Proctor, Bob, and Sandra Gallagher. The Art of Living. New York City, New York : Tarcher, 2016.

47. Whole. This Is Us 1, no. 1. New York , New York : NBC, 2016.

48. Johnson , Samuel. Forbes, 2024. https://www.forbes.com/quotes/8387/.

49. Glassman, Charles F. "Be Calm yet Assertive Quote." Goodreads, 2024. https://www.goodreads.com/.

50. Rumi. "Rumi Quote." Goodreads, 2024. https://www.goodreads.com/.

51. Vallely, Andrea. "'The Path to Freedom Is Not to Take Life so Seriously,'" Shift Happens. Accessed March 5, 2024. https://shifthappens.global/.

About the Author

Lee Vallely is a seasoned transformational coach with over twenty-four years of experience in empowering individuals to overcome phobias and anxieties. Despite grappling with social anxiety for most of his life, Lee has become a beacon of inspiration and success in the field.

Originally from the UK, Lee has an impressive 100 percent success rate in curing phobias, with a singular misadventure in the USA, that's spoken about in the book.

Lee's journey is as compelling as the transformations he facilitates.

Beyond his expertise in phobia cures, Lee has left an indelible mark in the health and fitness world. His work with young, elite tennis players on mental toughness has propelled them to remarkable levels of success. Previously being a personal trainer, nutritional advisor, and an NLP trainer, he seamlessly incorporates his wealth of knowledge into dynamic seminars and personal coaching sessions.

Lee's impact extends to the world of motivational giants, where he served as a leader for Tony Robbins, Paul McKenna, Richard Bandler, the co-founder of NLP, and facilitated for Bob Proctor, the narrator of *The Secret* film. It's remarkable that, even while confidently addressing mental health topics on *CBS News* and speaking on stage to thousands, Lee grappled with social anxiety personally.

In this captivating book, Lee candidly shares his transformative journey, unraveling the missing link that liberated him from social anxiety. Now he is living life to the fullest and finally feeling at ease in his own skin. His story is not just a testament to overcoming personal struggles, but an invitation for others to break free and embrace the joy of living.

You can contact Lee: www.shifthappens.global or email: lee.vallely@yahoo.com

If Lee is not in the coffee shop writing, or facilitating, he's either sweating in yoga or hanging out with Snowy, his (not his wife's) cat.

Get your free download of the meditation that accompanies this book. This meditation, when used on a regular basis (it is recommended that you use twice per day for twenty-eight days), will download the belief system to help create new neural pathways so that you start to think like the person that you want to be, while breaking down the old beliefs that were not serving you: https://shifthappens4u.kartra.com/page/Wai1532